AF255227

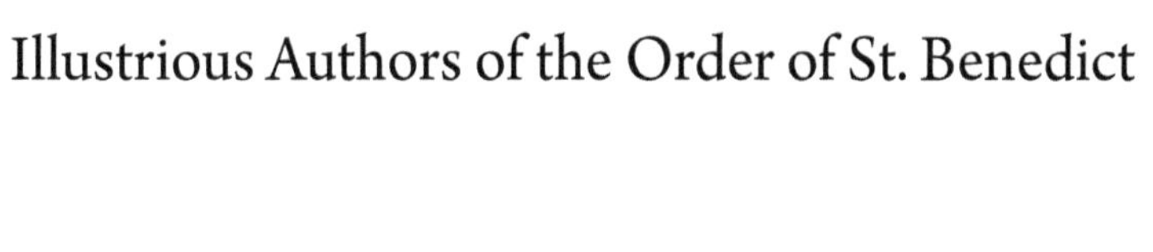

Illustrious Authors of the Order of St. Benedict

Illustrious Authors of the Order of St. Benedict

BY

Johannes Trithemius

TRANSLATED BY

Robert Nixon

WIPF & STOCK · Eugene, Oregon

A monk who is a lover of the sacred writings is like a lion,
the strongest of all beasts, who fears no enemies.

—Johannes Trithemius

Contents

Translator's Introduction

In many respects, the Benedictine abbot Johannes Trithemius (1462–1516) was an almost exemplary figure of the Renaissance polymath. Described as a man "of peerless intelligence, and a radiant beam of all erudition in his own age, most fertile though it was in extremely learned men,"[1] he was expert in a bewilderingly diverse variety of disciplines. His voluminous writings encompass the disciplines of history, theology, philosophy, scripture, spirituality, canon law, secular literature, ancient languages, medicine, the natural sciences, mathematics, cryptography, and occult studies.

Yet it is as an encyclopedist of ecclesiastical writers that he is most frequently cited, and it is through his work in this field that he has made his most enduring and valuable contribution to scholarship. Indeed, anyone who has explored the venerable tomes of Baronius, the Bollandists, Mabillon, and Migne, will immediately recognize the virtual ubiquity of the name of Trithemius as a respected reference. In this context, he appears as an apparently inexhaustible source of information on the lives and works of the earlier writers of the church. Although he was necessarily limited by the scope and accuracy of the data and resources available to him, his catalogues of ecclesiastical writers are, on the whole, remarkable both for their comprehensiveness and accuracy, when judged by the standards of the day.

Johannes Trithemius was born in 1462 in Trittenheim, a town on the banks of the Moselle River in the diocese of Trier. It is from this town that he received his cognomen. His father passed away while he was an infant, and (as a result of various domestic hardships) the young Johannes was compelled to pursue his literary

---

1. Heidel, "Epistola Dedicatoria Damiano Hartardo," unnumbered page.

studies under the cover of secrecy and against the wishes of his tyrannical and violent stepfather. It is related that at night, when all the other members of his household had fallen asleep, he would creep out of his house to visit a friend who would instruct him in reading and writing. His progress was so rapid that within the space of a month of commencing his studies, he had thoroughly mastered the art of reading German vernacular texts.[2]

In 1482, inspired by an ardent desire to advance his literary education, he fled from his family home, travelling first to Trier then to Heidelberg. But one night he was caught outside in a heavy snowstorm, in the vicinity of the Benedictine abbey at Sponheim. He sought refuge in the monastery, and it was there that he came to embrace the monastic life,[3] taking the monastic habit on the day of his twentieth birthday.[4] Almost incredibly, within approximately a year of his admission as a novice monk, he was elected abbot of the same monastery. This election to the abbatial office followed the date of his profession by only eight months and seven days.[5]

During his tenure as abbot, he worked vigorously to improve the temporal, intellectual, and spiritual well-being of the monastery, particularly by enriching and expanding its library. However, in 1506 he departed from Sponheim, leaving (as he himself testifies) of his own free well, in response to "injuries done to him by the envious."[6] Shortly after this, he accepted the abbacy of St. James Abbey in Würzburg, occupying this position for the remainder of his life. His death in 1516 was, according to contemporary reports, received "with mourning and weeping by all learned persons, and indeed by the emperor himself and many princes."[7]

A number of studies of Trithemius have been published featuring detailed biographical information, and insightful portrayals of the many-faceted and complex character and activities

---

2. Heidel, "Vita Trithemii," unnumbered page.

3. Heidel, "Vita Trithemii," unnumbered page.

4. Duraclus, "Pinax," 4.

5. Heidel, "Vita Trithemii," 13.

6. Trithemius, "Chronicon Monasterii Sancti Jacobi," 15.

7. Trithemius, "Chronicon Monasterii Sancti Jacobi," 17.

of this learned abbot. Foremost among these are the German-language volume by Klaus Arnold, *Johannes Trithemius: 1462–1516*, and the English-language work by Noël L. Brann, *The Abbot Trithemius: The Renaissance of Monastic Humanism*. Both of these studies are reliable and well balanced, and informed by thorough surveys of the extant primary source material.

The well-known and much-discussed question of the involvement of Trithemius in the practice of sorcery lies beyond the scope of this brief introduction. Works of his such as his *Antipalus Maleficiorum, Steganographia, Polygraphia,* and *De Septem Secunda Deis id est Intelligentiis sive Spiritibus Moventibus Orbes* demonstrate quite clearly that he had a detailed familiarity with the lore and literature of both "angelic magic" and witchcraft (both of a popular and more learned variety). And there is a rather fantastic story (which was widely circulated and credited in its time, and apparently well attested) that when the Emperor Maximilian I was grieving for his recently deceased wife, Mary of Burgundy, Trithemius summoned up her ghost in order to comfort the bereaved monarch. Maximilian, however, far from being consoled, was appalled and terrified at the spectral apparition of his beloved spouse and sternly forbade the precocious and well-intentioned (but manifestly misguided) young abbot from ever repeating such a procedure in his presence.[8]

More convincing evidence of his involvement in esoteric learning is perhaps the fact that he was the mentor, confidante, and correspondent of the mysterious Cornelius Agrippa (the author of the notorious *De Occulta Philosophia Libri Tres*), and close friend of the real-life protype of the fictional Faust (i.e., Johann Fust, a printer, moneylender, and business partner of Gutenberg). But his knowledge and expertise in such matters does not, in itself, constitute definite evidence of any actual practice of the necromantic arts. Furthermore, some of the occult and alchemical works attributed to Trithemius (especially those that exist only in English versions) are

---

8. Godelmann, *Tractatus de Magis,* 36.

almost certainly spurious, both exploiting as well as perpetuating his Faustian persona in the popular imagination.[9]

As has been noted, Trithemius was a zealous lover of libraries and a passionate bibliophile. According to his student and friend Johannes Duraclus, he was "the greatest lover and worshipper of books, above all others whom I have ever known living in the flesh," and was always occupied with "reading and writings, both day and night."[10] When he was first elected abbot at Sponheim, its library consisted of a mere forty-eight volumes, but by the time he departed it had been expanded (largely thanks to his tireless efforts) to over two thousand tomes.[11] He is said often to have related how he expended over two thousand florins on the purchase of books—all from donations made to him by the nobility, and not from the monastery's own resources.[12] He embraced the newly developed technology of printing with whole-hearted enthusiasm, as heralding a golden era of ready access to books.[13] But he also firmly believed in the retention of monastic *scriptoria*, for the sake of the spiritual and intellectual benefits resulting from the diligent copying of texts by hand.[14]

Both the life and the writings of demonstrate that the love of learning and literature was central to Trithemius's vision of the monastic charism. In book 1 of *De Viris Illustribus Ordinis Sancti Benedicti* he writes of this with glowing and ebullient enthusiasm:

> Apart from the praying of the divine office, the rest of the time [of Benedictine monks and nuns] was devoted to the study of holy writings. For by such study not only is the

9. See, for example, Trithemius, *Veterum Sophorum Sigilla*. See also Trithemius, "Magic and Philosophy of Trithemius." In the case of the former work, the attribution of the work to the hand of Trithemius is apparently reliable, but it seems that he was only copying tracts already in circulation. See Trithemius, *Magical Amulets*, x.

10. Duraclus, "Pinax," 6–7.

11. Busaeus, "Historica Relatio."

12. Duraclus, "Pinax," 6–7. Two thousand German florins was the equivalent of almost five hundred ounces of gold.

13. Trithemius, *De Viris Illustribus* 2.145.

14. Trithemius, *De Laude Scriptorum*.

intellect illuminated, but the emotions are also moved to compunction. In this holy exercise of monks and nuns, the fire of love always sprang up, which called them to studious reading and vigilance in prayer. Those who devoted their attentions to reading of the sacred texts, would, in their free hours, apply themselves to writing commentaries and expositions of the same texts. Thus they produced books and treatises which encouraged the efforts and intentions of their brethren to seek after God. But, in accordance to the Rule, the other monks who were not capable of composing books did not give themselves over to idleness. Rather, after prayer, they dedicated themselves diligently to the manual task of copying books by hand. They transcribed works written by learned persons, which were apt for their times, and thus, from the original manuscripts, made these works available to the entire world. Others worked skillfully in the binding of volumes, others made corrections to copies, while others decorated volumes by rubrication. Thus there was no hand of any monk which did not participate in some way in the work of producing books![15]

It was his fervent literary enthusiasm (combined with his prodigious memory and indefatigable industry) which made Trithemius uniquely qualified to compile his catalogue of illustrious Benedictine authors. His comments suggest that his listing of books is generally not made simply from copying inventories or library catalogues but from actual and familiar acquaintance with the material itself. When he makes mention (as he very often does) of "having seen" or "having read" particular books, or certain volumes having "come into his hands," it is obvious that he is speaking quite literally.

The present volume offers an English translation of the second book of the work, *De Viris Illustribus Ordinis Sancti Benedicti*. This monumental work consists of four books in total, the first of which deals with the origins, progress, decline, and attempts at reformation of the order; the second catalogues the illustrious authors of the order (from the time of Benedict until the late fifteenth century);

---

15. Trithemius, *De Viris Illustribus* 1.6.

the third lists Benedictine saints and canonized persons; and the fourth and final book describes the various popes, cardinals, archbishops, and bishops that the order has produced.

It is the second book, on the illustrious writers of the Benedictine order, that is by far the most interesting and useful to scholars of monastic studies and the literature of the Middle Ages.[16] The value of this work is twofold. First, it provides biographical and bibliographic details of each of the listed writers, which are of value and interest in themselves. Of course, Trithemius cannot be accepted as an absolutely reliable authority in these details, as he himself openly acknowledges.[17] But this is precisely where the second dimension of the work's value and interest for the contemporary student emerges. For it reflects authentically the state of scholarship at the time, in a manner that is both fascinating and illuminating. Trithemius was considered to be (and very probably was) the greatest living authority on medieval authors in the late fifteenth and early sixteenth centuries, and the veneration and respect which he enjoyed continued well into the centuries which followed. Therefore, the views of Trithemius on any particular medieval author are of the highest importance and interest to the scholar, even (and perhaps especially) when they are not entirely accurate or consistent with current views.

The existence of a manuscript copy of *De Viris Illustribus Ordinis Sancti Benedicti* dating from 1492 establishes that the work was written by that time.[18] Yet the author's own references in the work to his other (and larger) catalogue, *De Scriptoribus*

---

16. It is to be noted that Trithemius treats the question of which writers are "Benedictine" in a rather broad and not entirely consistent manner, which contemporary readers may occasionally find perplexing and capricious. Thus he includes in the present compilation St. John Damascene, whose connection with the Benedictine tradition is extremely tenuous at best. On the other hand, he excludes such an illustrious and universally respected author as St. Bernard of Clairvaux, reflecting the view in circulation at the time that Cistercians were quite distinct from the mainstream Benedictine tradition.

17. Trithemius, *De Viris Illustribus* 2.144.

18. See Kloss, *Catalogue of the Library*, 342.

Ecclesiasticis, proves that it is posterior to that work.[19] *De Scriptoribus Ecclesiasticis* was first published in 1494, but it bears a dedicatory epistle showing that it had, in fact, also been completed by 1492. Thus it is clear that *De Viris Illustribus* followed *De Scriptoribus* within the space of less than a single year, both being completed in 1492.

Despite this chronological proximity, there are noteworthy differences in the approaches of the two works (quite apart from the occasional significant deviations in historical details presented in them). Whereas *De Scriptoribus Ecclesiasticis* takes the form of a systematic, and occasionally rather dry, catalogue, in the second book of *De Viris Illustribus,* Trithemius favors a less formal and even colloquial approach. He admits with easy frankness when the name of a particular monastery or the titles of certain books have slipped from his memory.[20] Similarly, he relates his own personal reactions to certain books, in a manner not found in *De Scriptoribus.* An instance of this is when speaking of the commentary on the books of Kings by Angelomus of Luxeuil, Trithemius enthusiastically professes that "this work is so subtle, so mystic and so perfect in achieving its goal that I have never read anything that is like it!"[21]

De Viris Illustribus also includes certain colorful anecdotes about authors, which are omitted from *De Scriptoribus.* Notable examples of this are the story of the abduction of Lanfranc of Canterbury by robbers, and his humble concealment of his remarkable erudition for a number of years from his fellow monks;[22] or the stories of the apparitions of the Blessed Virgin to Herman the Lame[23] and Rupert of Deutz.[24]

Despite the completion of *De Viris Illustribus* in 1492, it did not appear in print until 1575, when it was included in a large

---

19. See Trithemius, *De Viris Illustribus* 2.preface and 2.119.

20. See Trithemius, *De Viris Illustribus* 2.39 and 2.143.

21. Trithemius, *De Viris Illustribus* 2.42.

22. Trithemius, *De Viris Illustribus* 2.99.

23. Trithemius, *De Viris Illustribus* 2.84.

24. Trithemius, *De Viris Illustribus* 2.109.

compilation, together with the commentaries on the Rule of Benedict by Juan de Torquemada and Smaragdus of Saint-Mihiel.[25] It was published a second time in the 1605 Cologne volume of the author's *Opera Pia et Spirituales.* The text presented in these two editions is identical (apart from minor variants in orthography and typographical abbreviations). It is this text which has been used as the basis of the present translation.

It is pertinent to offer a few comments on the translational approach that has been adopted. Proper names of persons and places have, as far as practical, been given in their anglicized equivalents, or their equivalents in the local vernacular. The exception to this is when a person is more generally known by a Latin name (such as Paschasius Radbertus) or when there is no standard anglicized or vernacular form available. When Trithemius gives a name with an unusual orthography, this has been altered to the more usual and recognized form (with the alteration acknowledged in a footnote, except when it is of an extremely minor nature).

Another translational issue arises from the fact that when Trithemius identifies a book, the distinction between the subject of the book and the actual book title is not always clear (especially given the absence of italics or inverted commas in the original typesetting). For example, a work might typically be identified as something like *liber de officiis divinis.* For the modern English translator, this could be validly rendered as either "a book on the divine offices" or "the book [entitled] *On the Divine Offices.*" The present translator has treated as titles those identifications that are well known or that obviously function as such. Other cases have been decided as seems to work best in each instance.

Trithemius makes extremely frequent use of litotes, such as describing authors as *non ignarus,* or books as *non inutilis.* In most cases, these have been converted to the appropriate positive descriptions, for the sake of idiomatic felicity.

It is to be noted that he uses the terms *sacra scriptura* and *divina scriptura* primarily in contrast to *secularis literatura.* It is clear that by *sacra scriptura* he means to signify the entire field of

25. Torquemada et al, *Regula S. Benedicti,* 427–535.

sacred studies, and not the biblical texts only. Accordingly, these terms have been translated without capital letters, often using "writings" or "literature" rather than "scriptures."

In the relatively few cases where very substantial errors occur (such as the confusion or confounding of identities, or conspicuous anachronisms or misattributions), these have been identified in footnotes. Other details (such as years of birth and death) are included in footnotes wherever their presence seems helpful. However, such observations and additional details are by no means comprehensive, nor are they intended to be. For many of the writers included in this catalogue, there is a very considerable body of reliable contemporary scholarship available, to which the interested reader or researcher is well advised to refer.

It is the sincere hope of the translator that this work may prove to be of genuine usefulness to students of medieval literature and monastic history, and may also advance what was the primary objective of Trithemius himself in producing this magisterial compendium—namely, the inspiration and encouragement of the love of study and sacred learning, especially among the sons and daughters of the Order of St. Benedict.

Robert Nixon, OSB

Abbey of the Most Holy Trinity,
New Norcia, Western Australia

ILLUSTRIOUS AUTHORS OF THE ORDER OF ST. BENEDICT

(Book 2 of *De Viris Illustribus
Ordinis Sancti Benedicti*)

BY

JOHANNES TRITHEMIUS

Preface

The [literary and scholarly] endeavors of our predecessors [in the Benedictine order] call the souls of their juniors to imitate them diligently. Indeed, those who follow benefit more from the examples of such persons than they do by any mere words of exhortation. Having completed our first book, in which we briefly described the beginnings of the order of our holy father Benedict,[1] we shall now apply ourselves to the second book. In this book, we shall deal with the authors who have adorned our order with their writings and have also sustained the holy church in a magnificent manner. I have, in part, extracted [the details of] these great persons from that large volume that I recently presented to Johannes, the Prince-Bishop of Worms;[2] [and also obtained information,] in part, out of the known writings of the authors themselves, which I have included in the catalogue that follows.

But let no one imagine that I have made mention of all the illustrious authors of our order, for that would be (for me at least) impossible. I have rather included only details of those whom I have at hand and about whose writings I am not significantly doubtful. There were (I am sure) a great many other illustrious writers, whose names are written in the Book of Life of the just. Such persons undoubtedly produced many writings in their own times, but which have not come to my notice. Of these I am unable to make mention in this work.

1. This refers to the first book of *De Viris Illustribus Ordinis Sancti Benedicti,* which deals with the origins, progress, and reformations of the Benedictine order.

2. Trithemius is referring to his monumental *De Scriptoribus Ecclesiasticis,* which endeavors to catalogue the writers of the church comprehensively. It was completed in 1492 and first published in 1494.

But I have not been idle in my efforts to obtain [copies and knowledge of those books] that have not been readily available to me. Yet my friends have been requesting that I complete this catalogue, which I have so long promised them. Concerning those whose times or dates I was not able to determine [with any precision or certainty], I have positioned them in what seems to be an approximately suitable place [in the broadly chronological sequence of authors adopted here].

Hence I beg and implore that my readers do not conclude that I have fallen into error [in such cases]. Indeed, whenever I have had no [sufficiently reliable] data at hand, I have preferred (wisely, I hope) to omit details altogether. And I have nowhere deliberately inserted anything at all of a [known] falsehood into these pages.

Everything that I include in this catalogue is taken either out of ancient histories or out of the writings of the authors themselves to which I had access. Now, as I set out upon the promised narration, I shall make my beginning with our holy father St. Benedict himself.

A Catalogue of Illustrious Authors of the Order of St. Benedict

§1. Benedict

Benedict, the leader and patriarch of monks and the magnificent founder of our rule of life, was born of noble parents in the region of Norcia. He was a man of the most holy manner of life, and illuminated with a spirit of prophecy. Blessed Pope Gregory has written his life with great eloquence, demonstrating it to have been filled with virtues, as can be discovered in his second book of *Dialogues*. Benedict founded our holy order first in Montecassino, in the year of our Lord 520. There he gathered a great multitude of monks and remained in that place until the end of his life (as we have already said at the beginning of the first book of the present work).[1] He composed a rule for monks, of great discretion and radiant clarity of language. And it is under this same rule that we monks rejoice to undertake our spiritual combat.

It is also said that he wrote some brief letters. Concerning these, I am not able to say anything with certainty. He died (as some maintain), in the year of our Lord 542, in the fifth indiction. But Marius Scotus, a monk of Fulda, believed otherwise, saying

---

1. Trithemius, *De Viris Illustribus* 1.1.

that he died in 601, in the fourth indiction, at around the ninetieth year of his life.[2] And this has the appearance of being true.[3]

§2. Faustus, Monk

Faustus, a monk and disciple of our holy father Benedict, was a great man in his morals and manner of life, and of considerable erudition in the divine scriptures. At the age of seven, he was entrusted by his parents to this holy teacher [Benedict] to learn the monastic life. Being well instructed by him in the fear of the Lord, he became a great imitator of his teacher.

He was sent into France with blessed Maur and fought for the Lord strenuously in the same monastery there for many years. After the death [of Maur] and at the request of many of his brethren, Faustus returned to Montecassino and wrote there a life of Maur in elegant language. [The veracity of] this life was confirmed by the authority of Pope Boniface.

Faustus flourished in the year 600.

§3. Cassiodorus, Abbot

Cassiodorus served as chancellor to Theodoric, the king of Italy, and then became a senator for the city of Ravenna. He was a man of the highest learning in secular literature and an outstanding philosopher and rhetorician. But when he heard of the fame and devotion of our holy father Benedict, he was immediately inspired by divine love. Disdaining the world, he became a monk in one of Benedict's monasteries. There, fervently desiring to serve

2. Trithemius explains that this opinion is based on Marianus's calculations of the years in which Holy Saturday (the day on which Benedict is believed to have died) would fall on March 21, the traditional date of his death. Trithemius, *De Scriptoribus Ecclesiasticis*, 77. However, this dating of Benedict's death in 601 seems beyond the bounds of realistic possibility, given that the year of his birth is universally given as 480 (a year that Trithemius himself has given in the first book of the present work. Trithemius, *De Viris Illustribus* 1.1).

3. In Latin: *Et verisimile est.* Trithemius does not give his reasons for this judgment.

God with all his heart, he devoted himself entirely to the study of sacred writings. He made such progress both in his reading of these works and writing commentaries on them, that he—in whom so much of both secular and sacred learning abounded—barely had an equal in his time.

The many brilliant works that he composed testify to his merits. Of these works, I have been able to find the following: a commentary on the whole psalter, in 150 tracts; a *Three-Part History,* in twelve books; *On the Reason of the Soul,* in one book; *On the Song of Songs,* in one book; *On Divine Reading,* in three books; a *Memorial of Divine Scriptures,* in one book; *Brief Commentaries on the Epistles of Paul,* in fourteen books; a commentary on the Acts of the Apostles, in one book; a commentary on Revelation, in one book; a *Catalogue of Roman Consuls,* in one book. He also composed treatises on grammar, dialectics, rhetoric, philosophy, mathematics, geometry, astronomy and music. He produced twenty-eight books of his letters to various persons, a book on etymology, and one on [rhetorical] tropes and schemata. Cassiodorus also composed many other works that have not come to my notice.

When he had reached that age of ninety-three, at the request of the brethren, he wrote a very elegant treatise on orthography, in which he presents rules and principles collected from some twelve different authorities.

Cassiodorus flourished around the year of our Lord 600.[4]

§4. Dionysius the Humble, Abbot

Dionysius was a Roman abbot, known by the cognomen of "the Humble." He was very knowledgeable in the sacred writings and also most expert in secular literature. He was outstanding at performing calculations and accomplished in geometry, as well as possessing mastery of both the Greek and Latin languages. His teachings enjoyed great authority among the early monks.

He produced a number of short works that are worthy of high regard, of which only a few have come to my notice. He wrote a

---

4. Cassiodorus is believed to have lived from around 485 until around 583.

book on the calculation of the date of Easter and produced a great cycle showing its date for some 532 years. He composed a number of letters as well. He translated works from Greek into Latin, including the writings of Proterius of Alexandria to Pope Leo [I] on the celebration of Easter, and the book of Gregory of Nyssa *On the Human Condition.* Finally, he wrote a Latin version of the life of St. Pachomius.

Dionysius the Humble flourished in the year of our Lord 570.[5]

§5. Columbanus, Abbot

Columbanus, who was Irish by birth, was the founder and first abbot of the monastery at Luxeuil. He was a man of outstanding merit and sanctity, and sustained many labors for Christ. When he was still a youth in a monastery in Ireland, he made such progress in his studies that even then he produced works worthy of respect. These [early productions] include a fine work in polished language on the whole psalter, in one book. He is said to have produced other writings, but of these I am unable to recall anything that has come to my notice.

He was a zealous and very distinguished preacher of the word of God. For the sake of the love of God, he left his beloved native land and became a pilgrim for Christ. Travelling through Germany, France, and Burgundy, he turned many away from sin by his words and example. He also founded many monasteries in our regions, as well as in Ireland.

Columbanus flourished in the year of our Lord 600.[6]

§6. Jonas, Monk

Jonas, a monk and disciple of St. Columbanus and an associate of blessed Gall, was studious in the divine scriptures and by no

5. Dionysius the Humble (*Dionysius Exiguus*) is believed to have lived from about 470 until about 544.

6. Columbanus is believed to have lived from 543 until 615.

means lacking in knowledge of secular literature. He was pure in his intellect and clear and confident in his eloquence.

He is said to have written the lives of many saints. Of these, I have been able to locate only the *Life of St. Columbanus*, his teacher, in one book; the *Life of St. Eustace*, who, after Columbanus had suffered exile, succeeded him as abbot of the monastery at Luxeuil, in one book; and the *Life of St. Attala*, a monk and disciple of Columbanus, also in one book.

Jonas flourished in the year of the Lord 630, under the reign of Heraclius.[7]

§7. Eugippius, Abbot

The abbot Eugippius was diligent in the study of all the divine scriptures and a most ardent reader and investigator of the books of blessed Augustine. He was of keen intelligence and a renowned orator. At the urgings of Randux, the bishop of Naples, he compiled a very useful anthology of the writings of Augustine to the virgin Proba. This book the bishop presented with his own hands to the church at Naples. Eugippius also wrote a life of the monk St. Severinus, in one book; and a *Rule of Life* for monks at his own monastery, in the form of an exhortation, likewise in one book.

If he wrote anything more than this, none of these other works have come to my notice. According to Sigebertus,[8] Eugippius lived during the reign of the emperor Tiberius Constantine and the pontificate of Pelagius II. He flourished in the year of our Lord 580.[9]

7. Jonas of Bobbio is believed to have lived from around 600 until 659. Trithemius is referring to the Byzantine emperor Heraclius I, who ruled from 610 to 641. In the absence of an emperor in Rome, Trithemius identifies the Byzantine emperor in this and several other cases that follow.

8. Trithemius is referring to Sigebertus Gemblacensis, who compiled a book on ecclesiastical writers in the eleventh or twelfth century.

9. Eugippius is believed to have lived from about 460 to about 535.

§8. Gregory the Great, Pope

Pope Gregory I had been abbot of the monastery of St. Andrew the Apostle in the city of the Rome, which he had founded himself. He was a man of the most holy manner of life and extremely learned in both sacred scriptures and secular literature. He was a distinguished philosopher and orator, whose eloquence was delightful and of remarkable beauty. The Holy Spirit seemed to open to him the profound sense of scriptures in visible form and to reveal to him hidden mysteries.

He produced many brilliant volumes of writings, which are enumerated below: a *Moral Commentary on Job,* to the bishop Leander of Seville (an extremely useful work and eminently worthy of all [possible] praise), in thirty-five books; two books of homilies on the first and final parts of the prophecy of Ezekiel; two books containing [a total of] forty homilies on the Gospels, addressed to the bishop Marianus; *On Pastoral Care,* to John, the bishop of Ravenna, in two books; four books of *Dialogues,* to the queen of the Lombards; the *Conflict of Virtues and Vices,* in one book; four homilies on the Song of Songs; a brief and succinct exposition of the four Gospels (which is a most rare work, able to be found in a very ancient codex in a certain monastery of our order); an explanation of the divine offices, in one book; one book of prefaces to the [books of] the New and Old Testaments; *On the Sacraments,* in one book; *Rules of Living,* to the newly converted Angles, in one book; and some thirteen books of letters.

He also composed many other works, which, however, the jealousy of the envious have consigned to the flames. These included works on the prophets, the five books of Moses, the books of Kings, and many others, as are mentioned by John the Deacon in his life of Gregory. This most blessed pontiff also produced an *antiphonale,* featuring delightful melodies. He authorized a missal, established scholas of cantors in Rome, and did many other praiseworthy things. Gregory died in the year of our Lord 603, in the sixth indiction.[10]

---

10. Gregory is believed to have lived from around 540 until 604.

§9. Leander, Bishop of Seville

Leander was a monk of our order who was made bishop of Seville, in the province of Baetica. By birth, he was African and his native city was Carthage, his father being Severianus. He was a particularly close friend of Pope Gregory [I], and it was at the request of Leander that that blessed pontiff wrote his great *Moral Commentary on Job.*

Leander was a man of holy and religious life and diligent in the study of the sacred writings. He was distinguished for his intelligence and an accomplished speaker. The entire Visigoth people were converted from the Arian error to the Catholic faith by means of his preaching and hard work.

Leander wrote many and varied tracts, in which his learning is amply displayed. Of these, the following survive: *Against the Heretics,* in two books; *Against the Beliefs of the Arians,* in one book; *On the Institution of Virgins,* to his sister, Florentia, in one book; two collections of beautiful homilies on the whole psalter; *On Baptism,* to Pope Gregory; *On Contempt for the World,* to his brother, in one book; and one book of his letters to various persons. He also composed a treatise in delightfully sonorous language, entitled *The Praises of Sacrifice,* and many other works that remain unknown. He flourished during the times of Pope Gregory [the Great], under the reign of the emperor Phocas,[11] in the year of our Lord 600.[12]

§10. Gregory of Tours

Gregory Florentius was a monk of our order, who became archbishop of Tours. He was a holy man, beloved by both God and the people. Gregory possessed the highest expertise in the sacred writings and was particularly diligent in studying the deeds of the saints.

On account of his great sanctity, he became known to Pope Gregory. This blessed pontiff received [Gregory of Tours] most

11. A Byzantine emperor, who reigned from 602 to 610.

12. Leander is believed to have lived from around 534 until 600 or 601.

reverently and acknowledged him to be a true saint, when he came to visit the thresholds of the apostles Peter and Paul in Rome. This we shall speak of in more detail in the third book of this present work, God willing.[13]

As a man of great education and learning, Gregory wrote many works in clear language. These include: an ecclesiastical history of the deeds of the Franks, in ten books; *In Praise of the Holy Martyrs*, in one book; the *Miracles of the Martyr St. Julian*, in one book; the *Miracles of St. Martin* (a former archbishop of Tours), in four books; and the *Lives of the Holy Fathers*, in one book. He also wrote numerous other books and treatises, which I have not yet seen.

Gregory of Tours flourished in the year of our Lord 600.[14]

§11. Claudius, Abbot

Claudius, an abbot at the monastery at Classe,[15] was a diligent student of sacred scriptures, and enjoyed close familiarity with blessed Pope Gregory [I]. He recorded many things which he had heard Gregory say, expounding the book of Proverbs, the Song of Songs, the Heptateuch, the prophets, and the books of Kings. These were things not written down by Gregory himself, on account of his infirmity [at the time]. But Claudius recorded the sense of them, lest Gregory's thoughts should be lost [to future readers]. When the pontiff [read these writings, and] came to know that many things had been [unintentionally] changed [in the written accounts], he studiously recollected his thoughts and carefully corrected the texts himself.

If Claudius wrote anything beyond this, it has not come to my notice. He flourished in the year of our Lord 600.

13. Trithemius is here referring to entry for Gregory of Tours in the third book of *De Viris Illustribus Ordinis Sancti Benedicti*. See Trithemius, *De Viris Illustribus* 3.52.

14. It is believed that Gregory of Tours lived from around 534 until 593 or 594.

15. An ancient port close to Ravenna.

§12. Haederic, Monk of Rome

Haederic was a monk of [the monastery] of Pope St. Gregory.[16] He burned with such an ardent love of Gregory's books that he regarded it as his highest delight to immerse himself in reading them. He was most studious in his studies of the divine writings and is said to have composed several short works in which his genius is amply displayed. There exists a great volume in which, with much care and labor, he compiled the best sentences from Gregory's *Moral Commentary on Job*. He flourished in the year of our Lord 640.

§13. Martin of Dumio, Bishop

Martin, who was born in the eastern parts of Gaul, served as abbot of the monastery at Dumio and was then made bishop of the Gallecians.[17] He converted the Suebi people from the Arian heresy to Catholic faith. He also composed a rule of faith and holy living, as well as restoring churches, founding monasteries, and promulgating many holy rulings. Among his other writings, he produced one book on the distinctions of the four virtues, addressed to Mito, king [of the Suebi], as well other works. He flourished in the year of our Lord 650.[18]

16. This is presumably the monastery of St. Andrew, of which Gregory was founder and first abbot.

17. The Latin text here reads *episcopus Galliarum* (bishop of the Gauls), but Trithemius almost certainly intends *episcopus Galleciarum* (bishop of the Gallecians). Martin was bishop of Bracara Augusta (now known as Braga), in what was then the province of Gallaecia. On the other hand, when Trithemius says that Martin was born "in the eastern parts of Gaul" (*ex partibus Orientalibus in Galliam*), he appears to be using *Galliam* correctly, as Martin is believed to have been born in Pannonia. In *De Scriptoribus Ecclesiasticis*, it is stated that Martin was a bishop, without identifying his diocese, perhaps reflecting Trithemius's recognition of his own uncertainty concerning the matter.

18. Martin of Dumio (i.e., Martin of Braga) is believed to have lived from around 520 until around 580. In *De Scriptoribus Ecclesiasticis*, Trithemius states (accurately) that he flourished in 540. Trithemius, *De Scriptoribus Ecclesiasticis*, 54. But the year given here does not seem to be a scribal or typographical error, as it accords with the approximately chronological ordering of authors.

§14. Eutropius, Bishop of Valencia

Eutropius was abbot of the Servitanum monastery[19] and bishop of the city of Valencia. He was learned in divine scripture and a zealous lover of the monastic rule, intellectually brilliant, and radiant in his eloquence. He wrote several works that are well worth reading. The few of these which have come to my notice include: *On the Baptism of Infants,* to Licinianus, bishop of Cartagena, in one book; *On Compelling Monks* [*to Observe Monastic Discipline*], in one book, and addressed to Peter, bishop [of Iturbica]; as well as many letters to various persons. He flourished in the year of our Lord 610.

§15. John, Bishop of Girona[20]

The most holy John was a monk who became bishop of Girona. He was of the nation of the Goths and of the province of Portugal. John was venerable for both his knowledge and doctrine, as well as his sanctity and manner of life. When he was a youth, his love of learning led him to seek the East. He resided in Constantinople for some seven years, applying himself with determination to the mastery of both Latin and Greek. Then, having attained an outstanding level of erudition, he returned to Spain. When the king, Leovigild, who was infected with the Arian error, was unable to prevail upon John to accept this same heresy, he sentenced him to ten years of exile. During this time, he endured a great many hardships and afflictions for the sake of his faith. When at last he was liberated from this sentence of exile, he founded a monastery at Biclaro and served the Lord there.[21]

He wrote an *Exhortation to Monks,* in one book; and a continuation of the chronicles [of Victor Tunnuna], also in one book.

19. This monastery was evidently located near Valencia.

20. This John is generally referred to as John of Biclaro, after the location of the monastery that he founded.

21. The location of Biclaro is uncertain.

He is said to have written many other works, which have not come to my notice. John flourished in the year of our Lord 610.[22]

§16. Caesarius of Arles, Bishop

Caesarius, who was monk and abbot of Lérins monastery before becoming bishop of Arles, was a holy and learned man, and an outstanding preacher. He was prompt and ready in his ingenuity and pleasing in his eloquence. His speech was distinguished by a beautiful diversity of style and expression, and a most convincing persuasiveness. He wrote attractive and useful sermons for the instruction of monks. Of these, we have read some twenty-two. In the third of these, he declares himself to be an imitator of our holy father Benedict, saying, "Meditating upon such [spiritual] matters, beloved brethren, and sweating in this battle [of the monastic life], we may know ourselves to be [true] sons and disciples of our holy father Benedict!"

The other works that he wrote I have not been able to view. He flourished in the year of our Lord 690.[23]

§17. Adomnán, Abbot

Adomnán, a priest and abbot of the monastery on the Scottish island of Iona, was an avid and accomplished student of the sacred scriptures and learned also in secular literature. He was cautious and careful in his mental disposition, pleasing in his speech, and venerable in his life and conduct. Moreover, he was the [spiritual] father of many thousands of monks.

Bede recalls him with praise in the fifth book of his *Ecclesiastical Histories*. Being a learned man and an expert in all fields of knowledge, Adomnán produced a work on the places of the Holy

22. John of Biclaro is believed to have lived from around 540 until sometime after 621.

23. Caesarius of Arles is believed to have lived from about 470 until about 542. This would obviously make the reference to Benedict that Trithemius has just cited seem highly doubtful, and it is not to be found in what are now regarded as his genuine sermons.

Land, in one book. He wrote also many other works, especially letters. He flourished in the year of the Lord 690.[24]

§18. Theodore, Archbishop

Theodore was a monk in Rome, but of Greek nationality. He was sent by Pope Vitalian to serve as the seventh archbishop of Canterbury in England. He was extremely learned in the sacred writings and most diligent in his observance of Catholic traditions. He convened a synod in England, which produced many useful results for the church.

In the fourth books of his *Ecclesiastical Histories*, Bede makes extensive mention and praise of Theodore's most holy endeavors. He wrote a book on penance of distinguished quality, which Gratian (the compiler of *Decretum*) often read [and referred to].[25] Theodore died in the year of our Lord 690, in the third indiction. He was then in the eighty-eighth year of his life and the twenty-second year of his episcopy.[26]

§19. Benedict, Abbot in England[27]

Benedict was abbot of the monastery of St. Peter and St. Paul in England. Bede, when he was seven years old, was entrusted to his guardianship and instruction by his parents. Benedict was diligent in his studies of holy writings and a zealous leader in the observance of the monastic rule. When he passed away, he was widely venerated as a saint.

He wrote a book for monks, which he called the *Concordance of Rules*.[28] In this work, he compared the rules of many [ancient

24. Adomnán is believed to have lived from around 624 until 704.

25. This Gratian compiled a *decretum* or collection of legislative documents in the twelfth century.

26. This Theodore is generally referred to as Theodore of Tarsus, after his place of birth. He is believed to have lived from 602 until 690.

27. This Benedict is known as Benedict Biscop.

28. This *Concordia regularum* is now attributed to St. Benedict of Aniane.

monastic] fathers with that of [our own] St. Benedict of Monte-cassino. He thereby demonstrated that [the Rule of Benedict] was in accordance with the various monastic rules which had preceded it and harmonized with all the ancient rules of the fathers. Benedict flourished in the year 670.[29]

§20. Ceolfrid, Abbot of the Same Monastery [of St. Peter and St. Paul, in England]

Ceolfrid became the abbot of the same monastery [of St. Peter and St. Paul, in England], after Benedict [Biscop, spoken of above]. Under his abbacy, Bede wrote many of his books. Ceolfrid, a most learned and devout man, wrote a number of letters to various persons, filled with erudition. Of these, I have read only that addressed to the king of the Picts, about the correct determination of the time of Easter. Through this letter, he satisfied the mind of the king on this matter and thus brought the Picts into harmony with the universal church.

Ceolfrid flourished in the year of our Lord 700.[30] Towards the end of his life, he made a pilgrimage to Rome, inspired by devout love of the apostles. On his way home he was accompanied by many pilgrims but was struck with illness at Langres.[31] He died there at the age of seventy-four, in the forty-seventh year of his priesthood and the thirty-fifth year of his abbatial office.

§21. Bede, Priest and Monk

Bede, a priest and monk of the monastery of the apostles St. Peter and St. Paul, was a student of both Benedict [Biscop][32] and Ceolfrid.[33] He was a studious scholar of sacred scripture and also

---

29. Benedict Biscop is believed to have lived from around 628 until 690.
30. Ceolfrid is believed to have lived from around 642 until 716.
31. In northeast France.
32. See §19.
33. See §20.

outstanding in his life and conduct. Indeed, he was one of the most important of the doctors [of the church].[34]

When Bede was seven years of age, his parents entrusted him to the said monastery. There he made astounding progress under the aforementioned abbots,and soon became a learned and most holy man. He devoted all the time of his life to the study of literature. And not only in sacred scriptures but in all the humane arts, he was most erudite. Never did he repine in idleness, as so many do today! Never did he cease from his studies. Rather, he constantly read, he constantly wrote, he constantly taught, and he constantly prayed. For he knew that the true lover of sacred learning easily overcomes the vices of the flesh.

Hence it was that he never accepted the office of abbot when it was offered to him, lest he become distracted by domestic concerns and thus be drawn from the embrace of his beautiful Rachel [(that is, his sacred studies)] or compelled to be separated from her. For had he became an abbot, he would not have been able to produce so very many or such wonderful books. For the abbatial office requires care, and care distracts the mind, and such distraction impedes the free pursuit of literary studies.

Bede wrote many brilliant works, in all forms and upon all subjects. These include his commentaries on Genesis, Exodus, Leviticus, Numbers, and Deuteronomy; his exposition on the beginning of the book of Kings, in three books;[35] and his work treating thirty questions pertaining to the book of Kings, in one book. He wrote also *On the Tabernacle and Its Vessels,* in four books; *The Building of the Temple,* in two books; a commentary on Joshua, in one book; on Judges, in one book; on the books of Chronicles, in two books; on the Proverbs of Solomon, in three books; on Ecclesiastes, in one book; on the Song of Songs, in eight books. Bede also produced a florilegium of the comments of blessed Pope Gregory on the Song of Songs. He wrote an exposition on the psalter, in one book; on Esdras and Nehemiah,

34. Latin: *non minima pars doctorum fuit.*

35. Trithemius seems to be referring here to Bede's *In Samuelem prophetam allegorica expositio.*

in four books; on Tobit, in one book; on Isaiah, in two books; on Ezekiel, in two books; on Daniel, in one books; and upon each of the twelve minor prophets, in twelve books.

He composed commentaries on the Gospels of Matthew and Luke, [each] in six books; on Mark, in four books; and on John. He wrote two books of homilies on Gospel verses, and one book of sermons on diverse themes. He produced fourteen books, treating all the letters of Paul; seven books on the Catholic epistles; four books on the Acts of the Apostles; and three books on the Apocalypse. He wrote a smaller volume *On Times*,[36] in one book; and a larger volume on the same subject, in two books. He compiled a volume, *Sparks from the Sentences of the Fathers*, in one book; a volume recording the deeds of certain saints, also in one book; a martyrology, in one book; the *Passion of St. Felix*, in one book; the *Life of St. Albert the Bishop*, in one book; a chronicle of his monastery, in two books; the *Ecclesiastical History of the English People*, in five books; a collection of hymns in different meters, in one book; readings from the Old Testament, in two books; readings from the New Testament, in two books; on orthography, in one book; on arithmetic, in one books; the *Art of Poetry*, in one book; on *Ecclesiastical Computation*, in one book;[37] and one book of letters addressed to various persons. He also wrote a great many other works, which have not come to my notice.

Even while he was still alive and writing new books, the works of this most erudite man were held in such authority and esteem that numerous bishops ordered them to be read publicly in churches and monasteries. Hence it came about that, since a person could not be given the title of saint while they were still alive, Bede was always referred to as "the Venerable" in giving his name as the author of his books. And this custom never ceased. And so it is that, even to this day, Bede is generally referred to as "the Venerable" rather than "St. Bede." However, there is no one

---

36. That is, upon the division of time, months, seasons, the ages of history, etc.

37. This perhaps refers to Bede's *De paschae celebratione liber*, dealing with the determination of the date of Easter.

who could doubt his sanctity. But the appellation by which he is identified on earth is of no consequence to one who reigns with all the saints in heaven.

There are those who assign other causes to the use of the title "the Venerable" for Bede; but he did not receive the epithet for the [spurious] reasons such persons propose. Nor was he blind, as some imagine. Bede died in the year of our Lord 733, in the first indiction, at the age of seventy-two.[38]

§22. Giles,[39] Monk and Abbot

The abbot Giles was of Greek nationality and a man of great erudition in the sacred scriptures, as well as extremely expert in secular learning. He was an accomplished philosopher, poet, and physician, excelling particularly in writing works in verse.

He wrote an outstanding work *On Pulses,* in verse, in one book;[40] and another in the same genre *On Veins,* also in one book. If he wrote any more than this, his other works have not come to my notice.

Many believe this Giles to have been the same sainted abbot whose feast is celebrated on September 1.[41] Whether or not this is so, I do not know with certainty. But I do know that the times and nationality [of the writer, Giles,] accord with those of [St. Giles the abbot]. Furthermore, there are not two monks of this name mentioned in the chronicles but only one. And it seems quite probable that St. Giles, before entering monastic life, practiced philosophy and medicine. He flourished around the year of our Lord 710.[42]

38. Bede is now believed to have died in 735.

39. Trithemius gives the name in its Latin form, Aegidius.

40. It seems that the book referred to here is *De pulsibus* by Gilles de Corbeil, a physician of the twelfth and thirteen centuries, whose *De pulsibus* had appeared in print 1485.

41. A certain Blessed Giles, a Spanish Cistercian abbot of the thirteen century, is venerated on September 1. Another St. Giles, an Umbrian hermit born in Greece, is also commemorated on the same day.

42. The year given here by Trithemius is obviously far removed from the times of either Gilles de Corbeil (the author of *De pulsibus*) or St. Giles the

§23. John Damascene[43]

John, a priest and monk of Damascus, Syria, was a man illustrious in both his manner of life and learning. Inspired by the writings of Pope Gregory II (whom many assert to have been a member of our order),[44] John wrote a sermon in Greek against the emperor Leo of Constantinople, who had attempted to forbid [the production and veneration of] images of saints. This sermon is a work of immense authority. He also wrote other works, which I have not yet seen. He flourished around the time of the same Pope Gregory II, in the year of our Lord 720.[45]

§24. Boniface, Archbishop

Boniface was a monk who became the first archbishop of Mainz. He was Scottish by birth[46] and a man of incomparable doctrine and sanctity. When he was still a boy of five years of age, he was entrusted by his parents to a certain monastery of our order, called Muschella.[47] After steadily progressing in merits, in due course he was ordained as a priest. He applied himself so diligently to the

---

Cistercian abbot, both of whom died in the thirteen century. It possibly refers to Giles, the Umbrian hermit, who is believed to have lived in the eighth century.

43. An editorial note in the 1605 Mainz edition reads: "Trithemius includes another [John] Damascene in his *De Scriptoribus Ecclesiasticis*, when there was only one, who was certainly not a Benedictine." Trithemius, *De Viris Illustribus* 2.23.

44. Interestingly, Trithemius himself does not include Gregory II in his catalogue of Benedictine popes (in book 4 of the present work). He does, however, include him in his listing of Benedictine saints (in book 3 of the present work). Trithemius, *De Viris Illustribus* 3.161. This inconsistency may reflect his own uncertainty about the question.

45. St. John Damascene is believed to have lived from around 675 until 749.

46. St. Boniface is believed to have been English by birth.

47. This monastery and location are otherwise unknown. The monastery is believed to have been located at Exeter.

study of divine writings that he was considered by all to be (and, indeed, was) a most illustrious teacher.

At last, inflamed by love of Christ and zeal for souls, and with the permission of his abbot, he became a pilgrim. Preaching the word of God, he made his way to Germany, where he converted many to the faith by his words and example. When the blessed Pope Gregory II heard of the power of Boniface's preaching, he ordained him as bishop of Mainz. The successor of Gregory II, Gregory III, bestowed upon Boniface the honor of the pallium and elevated him to the status of archbishop.

He was a most learned man and wrote short lives of various saints. Of these, I have been able to find only his life of St. Lebuinus. He produced one book of letters, addressed to Pope Zachary and various other persons. He also composed an outstanding work on the virtues and vices, adorned with verses.

At last, after many labors, Boniface was crowned with martyrdom, while preaching the Christian faith in Frisia in the year of our Lord 755, in the eighth indiction, in the thirty-sixth year of his episcopacy, on June 5.[48] His body was taken to Fulda, as he had previously planned, and there he was buried.

§25. Willibald, Monk

Willibald, a monk and priest, was a disciple of the blessed martyr Boniface, the archbishop of Mainz.[49] He was well versed in the sacred writings and by no means unlearned in secular studies, of sharp intellect, and eloquent in expression. And he was no less worthy of veneration for his devotion and virtue than for his learning.

Willibald wrote to Lullus, who succeeded Boniface as archbishop of Mainz, the life and passion of the same saint [Boniface],[50] in one book. He is said to have left other works displaying his great

---

48. Boniface is believed to have lived from around 675 until 754.

49. See §24.

50. I.e., Boniface.

intelligence, but these have not come into my hands. Willibald flourished in the year of our Lord 770.[51]

§26. Alcuin, Abbot

Alcuin, or Albinus, was the abbot of the monastery of St. Martin outside the city of Tours. He was born in Britain, and [later in his life] summoned [into service] by [the emperor] Charlemagne. Alcuin enjoyed such close familiarity with the emperor that Charlemagne referred to him as his "delightful master." And by means of his instruction, Charlemagne learned all the disciplines that are called liberal.

Alcuin was expert in both the divine scriptures and secular literature, and was held to be the most learned man of his times, in the opinion of all. He had been a disciple of the priest the Venerable Bede, in England. After the death of Bede, Alcuin, together with three other monks, went forth into France and then spent some time in the monastery at Fulda. He instructed many monks and produced a large number of distinguished students. Foremost among these were Haymo (who later became a bishop),[52] Usuard the monk,[53] and Rabanus Maurus.[54] Rabanus, who was still a boy when he was taught by Alcuin, was later to become a very great man.

In due course, by the decision of Charlemagne, Alcuin was appointed abbot of the monastery of St. Martin in Tours, where he shone forth for his sanctity and learning. Upon the orders of Charlemagne, he established a center for studies[55] in Paris (relocated from Rome), where he taught a great number of scholars, including many from among the monks [of the Benedictine order].

He produced many and varied works, including the following: *On Genesis,* in one book; *Questions on Genesis,* in one book;

---

51. Willibald is believed to have lived from about 700 until about 787.

52. That, is Haymo of Halberstadt. See §32.

53. The author of the famous martyrology. See §29.

54. See §39.

55. Latin: *stadium.*

On the Song of Songs, in one book; *Enchiridion on Certain Psalms,* in one book; *On the Epistle of Paul to the Hebrews,* in one book; *On All the Epistles of Paul,* in fourteen books; *On the Gospel of John,* in seven books; *On the Holy Trinity and the Catholic Faith,* to the emperor Charlemagne, in three books; *On the Nature and Immortality of the Soul,* to the virgin Eulalia, in one book; a *Compendium on the Virtues and Vices,* to Count Guido, in one book; a *Dialogue* to his disciples, in one book; *On the Revelation to John,* in one book; *On the Adoption of the Children of God,* in one book; *On the Blessings of the Patriarchs,* in one book; *The Life of St. Vedastus, Bishop,* in one book; *Questions on the Holy Trinity,* in one book; *On Church Doctrines,* in one book; the *Mirror of the Little Ones,* in one book; *On the Properties of the Names That Are Attributed to God in Sacred Scripture,* in one book. He also produced treatises on grammar, logic, orthography, music, astronomy, the art of poetry, handwriting, [poetic] meters, arithmetic and geometry, and rhetoric. There is a collection, in one book, of his letters to various persons, which are [however] seldom to be found collected together; and a *Prognostication Concerning the Future Age,* in one book. He also produced many other works, which have not come into my possession.

Alcuin flourished during the time of Charlemagne, in the year of our Lord 780.[56]

§27. John Scotus[57]

John Scotus[58] was a monk in England. He received teaching from the Venerable Bede, and was an associate and colleague of the aforementioned Alcuin. He was most learned in the sacred scriptures and also magnificently instructed in secular literature. John

---

56. Alcuin is believed to have lived from around 735 until 804.

57. As Trithemius includes the better-known John Scotus Erigena later in this catalogue of Benedictine writers (as John, abbot of Vercelli, §46), it is to be noted that the John Scotus referred to here was understood by Trithemius to be a different person.

58. The Latin term *scotus* includes both Irish and Scottish persons.

composed several short works that are worthy of respect. The few of these have come to my notice include: a commentary on the Gospel of Matthew in four books; and *On Human Duties,* in one book. But there are many others. John Scotus flourished under the reign of Charlemagne, in the year of our Lord 780.

§28. Claudius, Monk

Claudius was a monk, who is said once to have been a student of Bede and a colleague and associate of Albinus,[59] and was a man of the highest learning in all areas and expert in both the Greek and Latin languages. He is said to have written many works, including commentaries on the books of Genesis, Exodus, Leviticus, Numbers, Deuteronomy, Joshua, Judges, Ruth, and the Gospel according to Matthew. He produced numerous other works, which remain unknown to me. Claudius flourished in the year of our Lord 800.[60]

§29. Usuard, French Monk

Usuard was a French monk and is said to been a member of the monastery of Fulda, which is within the borders of the Franks.[61] He was a student of Albinus[62] and a most learned and studious man. At the command of the emperor Charles,[63] he compiled one volume encompassing the deeds and passions of all the holy martyrs, confessors, and virgins (in imitation of Eusebius of Caesarea[64]). This great work, the *Martyrology* of Usuard, has been

59. I.e., Alcuin.

60. It seems possible that Trithemius is referring to Claudius, bishop of Turin, who died in 827. Several of his commentaries on scripture survive (including a commentary on Genesis, Leviticus, the historical books, and the Gospel of Matthew). However, it is extremely unlikely he was ever a student of Bede or Alcuin.

61. Fulda is located in what is now the central German state of Hesse.

62. I.e., Alcuin.

63. I.e., Charlemagne.

64. That is, in imitation of the *Ecclesiastical Histories* of Eusebius.

preserved [in regular use] to the present day and continues to be read reverently in many churches.

I have been able to locate nothing of Usuard's other writings. He flourished under the reign of the same Charlemagne, in the year of our 780.[65]

§30. Paul of Lombardy, Monk

Paul of Lombardy was a monk of Montecassino and Italian by birth. Before his conversion [to monastic life] he had been a deacon in Aquileia and the personal secretary of Desiderius, king of the Lombards.

But it happened that the emperor Charles[66] took this Paul captive, together with King Desiderius, and led them both away to France with him. Very soon, the emperor came to hold Paul in the highest honor, on account of his outstanding intelligence. Indeed, he was greatly delighted by his eloquence and doctrine. Nevertheless, Paul was inspired by the Holy Spirit and came to look with disdain upon the world. He entered the monastery at Montecassino and showed himself to be a [true] monk, not only in the habit he wore but also in his manner of life.

He was an extremely knowledgeable man and produced many volumes of writings. These include: the *Deeds of the Lombards,* in six books; two books in continuation of the chronicles of Abbot Eutropius, written at the request of Aldeperga, the daughter of King Desiderius;[67] the *Life and Miracles of St. Benedict,* written in verse, in one book; the *Deeds of the Bishops of Metz,* in one book; the *Life of Pope Gregory the Great,* in one book; and the *Life and Miracles of St. Arnulf, Bishop of Metz,* in one book. At the command of [the emperor] Charles, he collected the lives and legends of the saints pertaining to all the feasts throughout the year. He also composed

65. Usuard is believed to have died around 877.

66. I.e., Charlemagne.

67. This refers to Paul's continuation of the *Breviarium historiae romanae* of Eutropius, entitled the *Historia romana.* Trithemius is mistaken in identifying this Eutropius as an abbot.

many hymns in various meters, including the sapphic hymn to John the Baptist, *Ut Queant Laxis.* Paul also produced many other writings, but these have not come to my notice.

There are some who write that he was summoned by Charlemagne from the monastery at Montecassino back into France, on account of his wisdom. He remained [so they say] for the remainder of his life in France, living in a certain monastery there and writing a great many volumes.

Paul flourished during the reign of the aforementioned Charlemagne, in the year of our Lord 790.[68]

§31. Hincmar, Archbishop of Reims

Hincmar was a monk of the monastery of St. Dionysius in Paris and afterward archbishop of Reims. He was extremely knowledgeable in both sacred and secular literature, subtle in his intelligence, and a skilled and highly persuasive orator. He wrote many works that are worthy of commendation. Of these, I have been able to find only the following: a *Life of St. Remigius, the First Archbishop of Reims,* in one book; an epitome of the writings of this same Remigius, in one book; and a letter to the church at Ravenna, written in the person of the emperor Charles, in one book. The other works that he produced have not come to our notice. He flourished under the reign of Charlemagne, in the year our Lord 790.[69]

§32. Haymo, Bishop of Halberstadt

Haymo was a monk of the monastery at Fulda, then served as abbot of Hersfeld, and finally became bishop of Halberstadt. He is said to have been a student of Albinus[70] and of the highest erudition in all fields of study. He was intellectually acute and an accomplished

---

68. Paul is believed to have lived from around 730 until around 799.

69. Hincmar is believed to have lived from around 806 until 882. He therefore lived under the reign of Charles the Bald, rather than of Charlemagne.

70. I.e., Alcuin.

speaker. And he was no less worthy of veneration for his sanctity of life than for his knowledge of the scriptures.

He wrote many brilliant volumes, which were held in great authority by scholars of earlier times. Of these works, I have been able to identify only the following: *On the Holy Trinity,* in one book; commentaries on the prophets Isaiah (in one book), Jeremiah (in one book), Ezekiel (in one book), and Daniel (in one book); commentaries on the twelve Minor Prophets, in twelve books; a commentary on the psalms, in one books; on the Song of Songs, in one book; on all the letters of Paul the apostle, in fourteen books; on the Catholic epistles, in seven books; on the Revelation to John, in one book; *On the Memory of Christian Matters,* in one book; and the *Varieties of Books,* in three books. He also produced a collection of homilies on the Gospels throughout the cycle of the year, filling two large volumes.

Haymo is also said to have written commentaries on the five books of Moses and [indeed] on the entire Bible. I believe that I once saw his commentary on Genesis.

It should not surprise you, O reader, if you find his name written in many varied ways in different manuscripts. For even if his name is given in different forms according to the diversity of languages, both with the Saxons and with us (such as Haymo, Heumo, or Hemmo), nevertheless we speak of one and the same person.

He died in the year of our Lord 834, in the twelfth indiction, in the fourteenth year of his episcopate.[71] He was buried in the great church of St. Stephen in Halberstadt and was widely considered to be a saint.

---

71. Haymo is believed to have died in 853.

§33. Aldhelm,[72] Bishop

Aldhelm was abbot of the monastery of Malmesbury in Scotland[73] and afterwards bishop of the West Saxons,[74] under [the metropolitan jurisdiction of] the archbishop of Canterbury. He was a holy and devout man and highly learned in both the sacred writings and the secular disciplines. He excelled especially in the composition of poems and songs. While he was still an abbot, he wrote (at the request of a synod of his nation) against the error of the Britons—specifically that they did not then celebrate Easter at its proper time and that they did various other things contrary to the peace and established customs of the church. By means of this volume, he drew many back into the peace of ecclesiastical unity. He composed also a great volume on the virginity of saints, written in verse; as well as letters to various persons.

Aldhelm also wrote many other works, as Bede testifies in the fifth book [of his *Ecclesiastical Histories*]. He was of outstanding learning, brilliant in his speech, and of astonishing erudition in both divine and liberal studies. His time as bishop lasted for only four years. Aldhelm flourished during the reign of King Pepin, the father of Charlemagne, in the year of our Lord 700.[75]

§34. Hilduin, Abbot

Hilduin was abbot of the monastery of St. Dionysius in Paris. It was to him that Rabanus Maurus, who was abbot of Fulda, dedicated his commentary on the books of Kings.[76] Hilduin was learned in the sacred scriptures and no less expert in the secular disciplines.

72. Trithemius gives the name in the form Adelmus.

73. Malmesbury is located in southwest England. However, it was founded by an Irishman (a *scotus*), Maildubh, who taught Aldhelm and whom Aldhelm succeeded as abbot. Trithemius refers to the abbey as *Maildubensis*, a name derived from that of its founder. The name Malmesbury seems to have evolved from this earlier appellation.

74. Aldhelm was bishop of Sherborne, in southwest England.

75. Aldhelm is believed to have lived from around 639 until 709.

76. See §39.

He was precise in his understanding and an effective speaker. It is said that he wrote a few works, in which he shows himself to be a man of outstanding learning; but not many of these have come to my notice. Indeed, I have found only one item of his—a great work, composed in both idioms of writing (that is, prose and verse), to Louis, the son of Charlemagne, on the life of St. Dionysius of Paris. Hilduin flourished in the year of our Lord 840.[77]

§35. Walafrid,[78] Abbot

Walafrid, the abbot of St. Gall, was German by birth, learned in the sacred writings, and extremely expert in secular literature. He was a magnificent rhetorician, an illustrious poet, and a strenuous monastic ruler. He composed a life of St. Gall in prose, in one book; and later, wrote the life of the same saint in verse, in one book. He also wrote a treatise *On the Divine Offices*, in one book; and several other works that are not known to us.

§36. Wandelbert, Monk

Wandelbert was a deacon and monk of the monastery at Prüm in the diocese of Trier. He was German by birth, learned in the sacred scriptures, and very well educated in secular literature. He was a renowned orator and brilliantly distinguished for his public speaking. At the behest of his abbot, Markward, he composed the *Life and Miracles of St. Goar, Confessor,* in one book. He wrote, for the same [Abbot Markward], a work on the miracles of St. Goar that had taken place in his own time, in one book. Wandelbert also wrote a martyrology in verse, covering the whole cycle of the year, in one book. He produced many other writings, but these have not

77. Hilduin is believed to have lived from about 785 until about 855.

78. This Walafrid is the same person as the writer whom Trithemius identifies as Strabo (see §41). He is normally known as Walafrid Strabo.

come to my notice. He flourished during the reign of the emperor Lothair,[79] in the year of our Lord 854.[80]

§37. Freculf, Bishop

Freculf was a monk of Fulda who later became bishop of Lisieux, under the metropolitan jurisdiction of the archbishop of Rouen. It was to him that Rabanus Maurus dedicated his four-book commentary on Genesis.[81] Freculf was a scholarly and learned man, and no less admirable for his piety than his knowledge. He wrote a magisterial work dedicated to Elisachar, presenting a history from the beginning of the world until the birth of Christ. In this work, he dealt with questions pertaining to difficult historical matters that arise in the scriptures.[82] He wrote a number of letters that should not be overlooked and other works that are unknown to me. He flourished in the year of our Lord 840.[83]

§38. Ratbod, Bishop

Ratbod, the bishop of Trier, was elevated from the habit and conversion of a monk to the episcopacy. He was both learned and holy, an outstanding preacher, and of subtle understanding and distinguished eloquence. Among the other writings in which his ingenuity is displayed, he wrote the lives of several saints and some useful homilies and sermons. He composed a *Life of St. Amelberga, Virgin*, in two books; and certain other works that are unknown to us. His memory is venerated among the saints.

79. I.e., Lothair I.

80. Wandelbert is believed to have lived from 830 until after 850.

81. See §39.

82. The work referred to here is the first tome of Freculf's *Chronicorum*, which covered the period mentioned and includes a dedicatory preface to Elisachar. Elisachar was abbot of the monastery of St. Maximim in Trier and is believed to have taught Freculf.

83. Freculf is believed to have died in about 850.

§39. Rabanus Maurus, Archbishop

Rabanus Maurus Magnentius served as abbot of the monastery at Fulda and was then appointed as sixth archbishop of Mainz. He was a German by nationality and born within the boundaries of the Franks, in the forest known as Buchonia, which is about fifteen miles from Mainz towards Thuringia. A former student and disciple of Albinus,[84] he was most knowledgeable of the sacred writings, with expert mastery also in all fields of secular learning. As a philosopher and poet, he was inferior to none of his contemporaries.

When Rabanus was still a boy, he was entrusted by his parents to Fulda monastery. There he made such progress in his studies that, in due course, there was no teacher in Germany who could equal him. Then, owing to the merits of his doctrine, he was unanimously chosen as abbot by the monks of his community. He served in that role for some twenty-four years, strenuously promoting monastic discipline.

He wrote a great many volumes, of which I have been able to locate the following: *On Genesis,* to Freculf of Lisieux,[85] in four books; *On Exodus,* in four books; *On Leviticus,* in four books; *On Numbers,* in four books: *On Deuteronomy,* in four books; *On Joshua,* in two books; *On Judges,* in two books; *On Ruth,* in one book; *On the Books of Kings,* dedicated to Hilduin,[86] in four books; *On the Books of Chronicles,* in four books; *On Esdras and Nehemiah,* in three books; *On Tobit,* in one book; *On Judith,* in seven books; *On Esther,* in one book; *On Job,* in one book; *On the Psalms,* in one book; *On the Proverbs of Solomon,* in one book; *On Ecclesiastes,* in one book; *On the Song of Songs,* in one book; *On the Book of Wisdom,* in one book; *On Ecclesiasticus,* in ten books; *On the Prophet Isaiah,* in eight books; *On Jeremiah,* in twenty books; *On Ezekiel,* in twenty books; *On Daniel,* in three books; *On the Twelve Minor Prophets,* in twelve books; *On Maccabees,* in three books; *On the Gospel of Matthew,* in eight books;

84. I.e., Alcuin.
85. See §37.
86. See §34.

On Mark, in three books; *On Luke,* in four books; *On John,* in one book; *On the Letters of Paul,* in twenty books; *On the Acts of the Apostles,* in one book; *On the Canonical Epistles,* in seven books; *On the Revelation to John,* in one book.

When he was thirty years of age and still a monk, he wrote a work that merits the highest possible admiration—namely, his marvelous poems *In Praise of the Holy Cross,* in two books. The first book is composed in verse, while the second book is in prose. Rabanus reverently offered this work to St. Peter, through the hands of [his successor], Pope Sergius. He wrote for Haymo, the bishop of Halberstadt,[87] his *Etymologies* or *On the Universe,* in twenty-two books; and for the same [Haymo], he wrote *On the Nature of the Universe,* in one book. For Haistulf, the fourth archbishop of Mainz, he wrote *On the Institution of Clerics,* in three books. For the bishop Heribert, he wrote *Questions on Canons,* in one book. For Regenbald, he wrote one book on the same subject [of questions on canons]. [Other works of his include:] *On the Blessings of the Patriarchs,* in one book; *On the Divine Offices,* in one book; and *On Ecclesiastical Computations,* in one (very useful) book. For King Louis, he produced a collection of his epistles to various persons, in one book. Rabanus also wrote sermons and homilies, which are virtually innumerable.

I have seen in the library of the monastery at Fulda many other books of Rabanus, mainly on the liberal arts. However, my forgetfulness has taken the titles of these from my memory at this moment. Among all the German and Italian teachers, there are none who equal him as a writer, either in the number of works he produced or in their usefulness. He certainly wrote a great multitude of works that we have not noted above.

Rabanus was a most scholarly and industrious man, always intent upon reading. He had many students who themselves became very learned men. He was the fourth abbot of Fulda (counting from St. Sturm, who was the first) and the sixth archbishop of Mainz, which office he filled for eight years. He was

87. See §32.

extremely merciful towards the poor, and in times of famine he exhibited to them great compassion, supporting many with the utmost generosity.

Rabanus died in the year of our Lord 855,[88] in the third indiction.

§40. Theodulf, Bishop

Theodulf, who was abbot of Fleury and then bishop of Orléans, was a man worthy of veneration for both his sanctity and learning. He is said to have produced several works, but I cannot recall any of them ever coming into my hands.

For some reason (of which I know nothing), he was incarcerated by the emperor Louis. While in prison, he composed the celebrated hymn *Gloria, Laus* [*et Honor*], inventing for it a most delightful melody. It is said that Theodulf was singing this in a loud voice [from his prison cell], and when the emperor chanced to be passing by he heard it. And he was so delighted and pacified by its wonderful sweetness that he immediately granted Theodulf his freedom. It is the laudable custom of the church to sing this hymn every year on Palm Sunday.

There were more than a few people who regarded this Theodulf as a saint. He flourished in the year of our Lord 840.[89]

§41. Strabo,[90] Monk of Fulda

Strabo, a monk of the monastery at Fulda and a German by birth, was once a student of Rabanus Maurus and served him as his scribe. He was a man of noble erudition. Instructed by such a good teacher [as Rabanus], he thoroughly mastered the divine scriptures.

---

88. Rabanus Maurus is believed to have lived from around 780 until 856.

89. Theodulf of Orléans is believed to have lived from about 750 until 821.

90. This is the same writer as the Walafrid (§35). Strabo (meaning "squint-eyed") was his cognomen.

Strabo produced numerous writings, which are all worth reading. These include commentaries on Genesis, Exodus, Leviticus, and many other books of the Bible. He is said to been the compiler of the *Glossa ordinaria* on the whole Bible, drawing from the works of the old fathers.[91] This is a work of the highest utility, whose value far exceeds any praise that might be conferred upon it.

Strabo was, as we have said, a disciple and scribe of Rabanus Maurus. He wrote out many of his works, thereby bringing them forth to the world. With Rabanus teaching him, Strabo became a man of the very highest learning. He flourished in the year of the Lord 840.[92]

§42. Angelomus, Monk

Angelomus, a monk of Luxeuil, was a man of sublime and exalted intelligence in the exposition of divine scriptures, and no less learned in secular than sacred literature. He wrote many great volumes, but few of these have come to our hands.

At the request of Drogo, bishop of Metz, of our order (who was the son of the emperor Charlemagne), he wrote an exposition of the books of Kings, in four books. This work is so subtle, so mystic, and so perfect in achieving its goal that I have never read anything that is like it!

Angelomus wrote for the emperor Louis[93] (who was the brother of Drogo) a commentary on the Song of Songs, in one book; and a treatise *On the Divine Offices,* also in one books. He flourished during the reign of Louis, the son of Charles,[94] in the year of our Lord 840.[95]

---

91. This erroneous attribution of the *Glossa ordinaria* to Walafrid Strabo seems to have gained currency from Trithemius himself.

92. Walafrid Strabo is believed to have lived from around 808 until 849.

93. I.e., Louis the Pious.

94. I.e., Charlemagne.

95. Angelomus is believed to have died in around 895.

§43. Amularius Fortunatus, Archbishop

Amularius, a monk of Luxeuil and afterwards archbishop of Trier, was extremely learned in the sacred scriptures, comprehensively instructed in secular literature, and venerable for his life and conduct. Such was his wisdom and eloquence that when he was sent to Constantinople by Charles[96] to see the emperor Michael, he successfully negotiated peace between [the two emperors].

He is said to have written a number of books that are filled with erudition. Among these are: *On Ecclesiastical Offices,* in one book; another work that treats the same subject more broadly, to Louis,[97] the son of Charles, in four books; and *On the Mysteries of the Mass,* in one book. If he wrote anything more than this, these other works have not yet come to my notice.

He flourished under the reign of the emperors Charlemagne and Louis, his son, in the year of our Lord, 830.[98]

§44. Florus, Monk of St. Trudo

Florus, a monk of the monastery of St. Trudo in the diocese of Liège, was a well educated man and most studious in the divine writings. Above all, he was a lover of the writings of St. Augustine, from whose sentences he made extensive compilations, congruent with his particular purposes. [In this way,] he produced an exposition of all the letters of the apostle St. Paul in such a magnificent manner that it can almost be seen as a work of St. Augustine himself. For he inserted into it nothing that was his own [but, rather, drew everything from the writings of Augustine].[99] Florus also wrote other works, none of which, however, have come to my notice.

96. I.e., Charlemagne.

97. I.e., Louis the Pious.

98. Amularius Fortunatus is believed to have lived from about 755 until about 850. He also served as archbishop of Lyon for a time.

99. This description of the writings of Florus (specifically, the Augustinian florilegium) accords with those of Florus of Lyon, whose biographical details, however, are entirely different from those given here. Florus of Lyon is believed to have died in around 860.

§45. Ansegisus, Archbishop

Ansegius, a monk of the monastery at Lobbes and afterwards archbishop of Sens, was an experts in all fields of learning and a close friend of the kings of his time. He was subtle in his intellect and prudent in his speech. He produced works that are useful in promoting the unity of the church and worthy of study.

Of these, I have read only the following: a compilation of the *Edicts of Charlemagne Pertaining to Ecclesiastical Law,* in two books; a compilation of the edicts of the same [Charlemagne] pertaining to secular law, in two books; the ecclesiastical edicts of Louis, his son, in two books; and the civil statues of the same [Louis], also in two books. I have seen none of his other writings.

Ansegius flourished in the year of our Lord 840.[100]

§46. John, Abbot of Vercelli

John Erigena, by birth a Scot,[101] was the abbot of the monastery at Vercelli.[102] He was a man of the most excellent intelligence and highly educated in both the Greek and Latin languages. At the request of Charles, the son of the emperor Louis and the brother of the emperor Lothair, he translated the books of Dionysius the Areopagite from Greek into Latin, also explaining them with his commentaries. He wrote *On the Division of Nature,* in one book, and some other works that have not come to my notice.

100. The years of birth and death of Ansegius are uncertain, but he became bishop of Sens in 871.

101. The term *scotus* includes both Irish and Scottish persons.

102. The description of John Scotus Erigena as serving as abbot at Vercelli is evidently inaccurate. Some sources relate that he was elected abbot at Malmesbury, but this is uncertain. Curiously, in the third book of *De Viris Illustribus,* Trithemius states that a John Scotus, who was abbot of Malmesbury, was martyred by his students, who stabbed him to death with their pens(!) in 880. He states there that this same John Scotus had been mentioned in the second book of the same work (apparently referring to this entry) but notes certain doubts about his identity, dates, and career. Trithemius, *De Viris Illustribus* 3.212. See also §27.

John [Scotus Erigena] flourished under the reign of the emperor Lothair[103] and his brothers, the kings Louis and Charles, in the year of our Lord 850.[104]

§47. Milo, Monk

Milo, a monk of the monastery of St. Amand,[105] was a man of the highest erudition in both sacred and secular literature. [The emperor] Charles[106] held him in high esteem and spread the opinion of Milo's great wisdom to place far afield.

Milo possessed keen understanding and was a skilled speaker. He was also an outstanding musician, rhetorician, and poet. He excelled in the composition of verse but also wrote praiseworthy works in prose. His writings include: *On Sobriety,* to Charles the Bald, in one book; *On Music,* in one book; and a *Life of St. Amand,* written in verse, in one book. Milo produced other works, too, but these are not known to me. He flourished in the year of our Lord 880.[107]

§48. Bertramus [Ratramnus],[108] Monk

Bertramus was a monk who was scholarly and erudite in the sacred writings and of distinguished education also in secular literature. He wrote a number of small works that should not be overlooked, in which his intelligence is displayed magnificently. Of these, I have been able to find only his treatise *On the Body and Blood of the Lord,*

103. I.e., Lothair I.

104. John Scotus Erigena is believed to have lived from around 800 until around 877.

105. In northern France.

106. I.e., Charles the Bald.

107. Milo of St. Amand is believed to have lived from around 810 until around 871.

108. The writer identified here as Bertramus is the same person as Ratramnus of Corbie.

in one book; and his work *On Predestination,* dedicated to Charles.[109] Bertramus flourished in the year of our Lord 870.[110]

§49. Hucbald, Monk

Hucbald, a monk of the monastery of St. Amand in Elnon, was of such expertise in all of the liberal arts that he was considered to be the equal of the ancient philosophers. He was an outstanding musician and poet and of extremely subtle intelligence.

He wrote many brilliant works in both verse and prose. Of these, I have been able to find the following: *The Deeds of St. Lebuin,* in one book; and *On Music,* in one book. He also composed a wonderful poem *In Praise of Bald Men,* comprising three hundred verses and dedicated to the emperor Charles the Bald. Now, every single word in this poem commences with the same letter! It commences thus: *Carmina clarisonae calvis cantate, Camoenae.*[111]

Hucbald wrote also the lives of many saints and composed various hymns and canticles with sweet and well-constructed melodies. He wrote letters to various persons, as well as other works with which I am not acquainted. He flourished during the time of Charles the Bald, in the year of the Lord 880.[112]

§50. Almannus, Monk

Almannus, a monk of the monastery at Hautvillers, was learned in the sacred writings and well educated also in the secular disciplines. He was renowned for his intelligence and eloquence, and an accomplished orator and poet. He wrote several works of not inconsiderable utility, of which, however, I have been able to locate only a few. These include: a *Life of St. Vinard, Archbishop of Reims,* in one book; a *Life of St. Sindulf,* in one book; and a *Life of St. Helena, the Queen,* in one book. He also wrote an account of

109. I.e., Charles the Bald.
110. Ratramnus (i.e., Bertramus) is believed to have died in about 868.
111. "O ye brilliantly resonant Muses, sing songs unto the bald!"
112. Hucbald is believed to have lived from around 850 until 930.

the translation of the body of the same [St. Helena] to his monastery at Hautvillers, in one book.

Because during his times France was devasted by the Normans, he composed (in one book) lamentations on the desolation of France and of his monastery, following the example of [the Lamentations of] the prophet Jeremiah. In these lamentations, he used a fourfold abecedarian form. He is said to have written other works, but these have not come to my notice. Almmanus flourished in the year of our Lord 890.[113]

§51. Adrevald, Monk

Adrevald, also known as Adelbert, was a monk of Fleury monastery. He was a learned man and widely admired in his time. He wrote many works, in which his intelligence is abundantly demonstrated. None of these, however, have come into my possession.

There is one book that he is said to have written, on the miracles of our holy father Benedict that happened in France at the time when his body was [supposedly] relocated to Fleury Monastery. Note, [O reader,] that there are some who claim that the body of our holy father [St. Benedict] was taken from Montecassino to Fleury by a certain monk called Aigulf. They attempt to prove [the authenticity of this supposed relocation] by citing virtually innumerable miracles. But the Italians, on the contrary, also claim that they have the body [of St. Benedict] and have always had it. And they produce no less evidence by citing an equally great multitude of miracles.[114]

Concerning these disputing parties, one may say (citing the verse of Horace): *Adhuc quod subjudice lis est.*[115] [And this would indeed be the case,] except that a certain Roman pontiff[116] was prevailed upon by the monks of Montecassino to prohibit anyone from ever daring to assert the body of Benedict has been moved. Hence

---

113. Almannus is believed to have lived from about 830 until about 889.

114. See Voragine et al., *St. Benedict's Bones.*

115. "The matter is still before the judge."

116. I.e., Urban II.

it is that the feast celebrated on July 11 is not called the Translation of St. Benedict but rather simply a commemoration.[117]

Adrevald flourished in the year 900.[118]

§52. Remigius, Monk of Auxerre

Remigius, a monk of the monastery at Auxerre, is said afterwards to have been made a bishop. He was knowledgeable of the sacred scriptures and regarded by all of his contemporaries as being an expert also in secular learning. He wrote many tracts on secular literature, expounding the works of the ancient authors. He also produced more than a few volumes on the divine writings.

The writings of Remigius include: *On the Song of Songs*, in one book; *On the Canon of the Mass*, in one book; *On the Divine Offices*; *On the Feasts of the Saints*, in one book; *On Two Questions*, to Edward (a bishop), in one book; and *On Donatus*, in one book. He wrote many other works, which have not come to my notice.

Remigius was the teacher of Odo, who became the abbot of Cluny, and a great many other illustrious men, whom he instructed well in all fields of divine and secular learning. He flourished during the time of Charles the Bald and died in the year of our Lord 980.[119]

117. The feast celebrated on July 11, traditionally of the Translation of St. Benedict, was not uniformly identified by this description, owing to ongoing disputes about the authenticity of the events commemorated.

118. Adrevald is believed to have lived from around 820 until around 879.

119. Remigius is believed to have lived from about 841 until 908. The year 980, given in the text and found in both the 1575 and 1605 editions, is almost a century removed from the reign of Charles the Bald. It also deviates strongly from the approximately chronological ordering of authors and is incongruous with the years given for Odo of Cluny, whom Trithemius states was a student of Remigius. Hence it seems likely that it is a scribal or typographical error. In *De Scriptoribus Ecclesiasticis*, Trithemius gives the year of Remigius's flourishing as 880. Trithemius, *De Scriptoribus Ecclesiasticis*, 68.

§53. Odo of Cluny

Odo, the abbot of Cluny, was once a student and disciple of Remigius of Auxerre.[120] He was a man most learned in all fields of sacred and secular studies, excelling in music, and no less distinguished for his sanctity of life. He served as chief cantor at Tours before he became a monk at Cluny. With the consent of all members of the community, he was elected as abbot there, following the death of [the previous abbot,] Berno. He was venerable both for his doctrine and holiness.

Odo produced writings of outstanding usefulness. Of these, however, only a few have come to my notice. This include: a brief chronicle of his times, in one book; a *Life of St. Gerard*, in one book; and *In Praise of St. Martin of Tours*, in one book. He is said to have composed many elegant sermons and homilies. He also composed hymns and canticles in honor of various saints.

Odo flourished in the 900th year after our Lord's nativity.[121]

§54. Regino of Prüm

Regino, the abbot of the monastery at Prüm in the diocese of Trier, was German by birth. He was learned in both sacred and secular literature and an outstanding historiographer and jurist. During his own times, he was regarded as the leading teacher among all the Germans. At the command of Ratbod, the archbishop of Trier, he compiled two books (comprising some nine hundred chapters) of decrees pertaining to ecclesiastical discipline and the Christian religion. For Adelberon, bishop of Metz, he wrote a chronicle, presenting principally the deeds of the French and Germans, from the birth of Christ until the year 908. He also wrote other works, which have not come to my notice. Regino flourished under the reign of Arnold (or Arnulf),[122] in the year of the Lord 900.[123]

120. See §52.

121. Odo is believed to have lived from around 878 until 942.

122. I.e., Arnulf II, duke of Bavaria (known as Arnulf the Wicked).

123. Regino is believed to have died in 915.

§55. Paschasius, Abbot of Corbie

Paschasius Radbertus, abbot of Corbie, was a man of the highest erudition in all fields. He was a master of both the Greek and Latin languages and was (according to the acclamation of all) the most celebrated theologian and philosopher of his time. His possessed an acute intellect, profound knowledge, and skillful speech. His writings are of considerable authority. Of these, I have been able to locate only the following: *On the Sacrament of the Altar*, to the abbot Placid, in one book; a *Life of St. Adelhard*, in one book; *On the Lamentations of the Prophet Jeremiah*, in one book. He translated some lives of the fathers from Greek into Latin and wrote some other works, which have not come to my notice.

§56. Erik, Monk

This Erik was a monk. Although I have searched, I have not been able to find out to which monastery he belonged. (There are some who claim he was a monk of Auxerre.) He was most learned in the sacred writings and well read in the works of the old fathers. He was also well educated in secular literature. He excelled in composing both verse and prose, and was an outstanding orator. His work in verse, *On the Life and Virtues of St. Germanus, Bishop of Auxerre*, in one book, is an admirable volume. Erik wrote also numerous sermons and homilies, copies of which are possessed by many. He is said to have written many other works, but these have not come to my notice.

§57. Ratherius, Bishop of Verona

Ratherius, a monk of Lobbes[124] who became bishop of Verona, was a man of marvelous simplicity but of great literary accomplishment. He was twice expelled from his episcopate, because he was seen to favor the Bavarians [excessively]. But each time [he was expelled],

---

124. In Wallonia, Belgium.

he was [afterwards] restored to his position. At last, he was made bishop of Liège but was also expelled from there!

He wrote numerous tracts, of which the following have come to my attention: *Against the Anthropomorphites,* in one book; his *Agnosticon* or *Praeloquiorum,*[125] in six books; and a volume of *Confessions,* in one book. When he was expelled from the episcopate at Verona, he wrote a book in which he laments his hardships with a certain facetious urbaneness. This book offers much that is able both to amuse and to profit those who read it.

When he was expelled from the episcopate at Liège, he wrote a book to which he gave the title *Frenzy.* Another work he wrote bears the title *Pointless Chatter*[126] (as he saw it!). He also produced a tract *On the Body and Blood of the Lord;* a treatise *On Predestination,* in two books; a *Life of St. Ursmar, Bishop of Lobbes,* in one book; and various other items, which I have not seen.

Ratherius died in the monastery at Lobbes, in the year of our Lord 974, in the second indiction. He was buried in this same place.

§58. Aimoin,[127] Monk

Aimoin, a monk of Fleury, was most studious and learned in the divine scriptures, and well informed also in secular literature. Encouraged by the example of Adrevald,[128] he wrote a continuation to [Adrevald's] history of the miracles of St. Benedict, adding many marvels that had taken place in Fleury and throughout France, until the times of Robert [II], that most learned king of France. He wrote other works also, but these have not come to my attention.

125. A collection of moral treatises.

126. Latin: *Ineffax garritus.*

127. Trithemius gives his name as *Amonius.* The usual Latin form is *Aimoinus.*

128. See §51.

Aimoin flourished under the reign of the aforementioned King Robert,[129] in the year 980.[130]

§59. Rupert, Abbot of Montecassino

Rupert, the abbot of the monastery at Montecassino, was extremely scholarly and learned in sacred literature. He was renowned both for his intelligence and his eloquence, and admirable for his sanctity of life and impeccable conduct. He was also a zealous lover of the discipline of the monastic rule.

Rupert wrote elegant sermons for the edification of his brethren. In his own times, these sermons were widely and studiously read. He produced other works, too, but none of these have come into my hands.

§60. Volquin, Abbot of Lobbes

Volquin, the abbot of Lobbes, was most learned and studious in the divine writings and also well educated in secular literature. He was characterized by mental alacrity and [was] a renowned orator. In particular, he was an expert on history.[131] At the request of his brethren, he wrote the *Deeds of the Abbots of Lobbes*. In this volume, he inserts many digressions, which are both entertaining and useful for the reader. He composed many sermons and homilies, in which his intelligence and character is displayed abundantly. Volquin also wrote other works, but these have not come to me.

§61. Widukind,[132] Monk

Widukind, a monk of Corvey abbey in Saxony, was a German by birth. He was a learned and eloquent man and highly expert

---

129. I.e., King Robert II of France, known as Robert the Pious and Robert the Wise.

130. Aimoin is believed to have lived from around 960 until around 1010.

131. Latin: *temporum cognitor.*

132. Trithemius gives his name as *Windichinus.*

in secular literature. In his time, he was famous as a teacher. He wrote a number of brilliant works, including the following: a *History of the Saxons,* until the death of Otto I, in three books; a *Life of St. Paul the Hermit* in both verse and prose,[133] in one book; the *Passion of St. Tecla,* in verse, in one book. He also wrote the *Life and Deeds of Emperor Otto I* for his [Otto's] daughter,[134] in one book. Widukind produced many other works, but these have not come to my notice.

In his time, many most learned men of our order flourished in Germany, especially in the monasteries at Corvey, Fulda, Hersfeld, and certain others. But [alas,] few writings of these men have come into my hands!

Widukind (who was also known as Windichild) flourished in the times of Otto II. He died in [about] the year of our Lord 970.[135]

§62. Abbo,[136] Abbot of Fleury

Abbo, abbot of the monastery at Fleury, was a man of holy life and a zealous lover of the discipline of the monastic rule. He was learned in the divine scriptures and well versed also in secular literature. He left many [literary] monuments of his intelligence. However, these have not come into our hands. There exists with us only a commentary [by Abbo] on the *Calculus* of Victorius,[137] in one book. I have been able to find nothing of his other writings.

After a great many labors in preaching, this most blessed man was encrimsoned with the blood of martyrdom.[138] He gave his life for his faith in Christ in Gascony, and thus entered into the

---

133. Latin: *alterno stylo,* indicating the presentation of material in both verse and prose.

134. According to the entry for Widukind in *De Scriptoribus Ecclesiasticis,* this daughter of Otto I was Mechthilde. Trithemius, *De Scriptoribus Ecclesiasticis,* 71.

135. Widukind is now believed to have died in about 973.

136. Trithemius gives the name as *Albo. Abbo* is the more usual form.

137. I.e., Victorius of Aquitaine.

138. Latin: *martyrio rubricatus,* i.e., "rubricated by martyrdom."

celestial kingdom. Abbo flourished under the reign of Otto II, in the year of our Lord 970.[139]

§63. Heriger, Abbot

Heriger was abbot of the monastery at Lobbes. Berno of Reichenau makes a memory of him in his book *On Advent*, dedicated to Aribo, archbishop of Mainz.[140] He was an extremely renowned man in his time, most learned in all fields of study and equally expert in both divine and secular writings. He was held in the highest esteem not only with the French but also with the Romans, Italians, and Germans.

He wrote many volumes, including: the *Deeds of the Bishops of Liège*, written in verse, in one book; a *Life of St. Usmar, Bishop of Lobbes*, also in verse, in one book. He wrote a dialogue, featuring himself as one of the interlocutors and Bishop Adalbold,[141] on discord within the church. He [also] wrote [a dialogue,] *On Advent*, which he sent to this same Adalbold, who was then residing in Rome. He addressed to Hugh (a monk) an epistle of *On Certain Questions*, in one book; and another one *On the Divine Offices*, similarly in one book. He also collected writings of the Catholic fathers against the views of Ratherius,[142] [entitled] *On the Body and Blood of Christ*.

Heriger also wrote many other works, but these have not come to my attention. He flourished during the reign of Otto II, in the year of our Lord 970.[143]

139. Abbo is believed to have lived from about 945 until his martyrdom in 1004.

140. See §77.

141. See §64.

142. See §57.

143. Heriger is believed to have lived from around 925 until 1007.

§64. Adalbold, Bishop

Adalbold was a monk of the monastery at Lobbes, who afterwards become bishop of Utrecht. It was to this Adalbold that Heriger[144] dedicated his dialogue *On Advent*. He was a man of the highest erudition in the divine scriptures and of distinguished expertise in secular learning. He was prudently cautious in his character, skillful in his speech, and devout in his life and conduct.

Adalbold is said to have written many works. Of these, only those noted below have come to my notice. First, there is his *Life of the Emperor St. Henry II*, in one book. Now there are some who claim that this emperor Henry should be called Henry I, because they believe that [the Henry who was] the son of Otto should not be numbered among the emperors, since he did not receive the imperial crown from the hands of pope.[145]

Adalbold also composed a work entitled *In Praise of the Holy Cross* and another called the *Praises of Holy Mary*, mixing both prose and verse. He wrote many other works, which have not come into my hands.

Adalbold flourished during the times of the [aforementioned] Henry [II], in the year of our Lord 1000.[146]

§65. Radulf, Monk

Radulf Flaviacensis, a monk of Fleury (as many claim), was a man of such learning and wisdom that in his time he had no equal in all of Germany, Italy, or France. In the divine writings he was most erudite and, as a philosopher, was second to none. Like another Augustine, he responded copiously to all who posed any question to him.

Radulf wrote a great many brilliant volumes. Of these, I have been able to find only the following: *On Leviticus*, in twenty

144. See §63.

145. The Henry referred to here, whose legitimacy as an emperor is doubted, was Henry the Fowler (876–936), the son of Otto the Illustrious, duke of Saxony.

146. Adalbold is believed to have lived from 975 until 1026.

books; *On the Letters of Paul,* in fourteen books; an addition to the chronicle of Eusebius extending to his own times, in one book; and a *History of the Deeds of the French and the Germans,* in one book. He is said also to have produced commentaries on many [other] books of the Bible, sermons, and various other tracts and epistles; but none of these have come into our hands.

§66. Osbern,[147] Monk

Osbern, a monk of Canterbury, was an expert in all secular literature and diligent also in study of the divine writings. He was an outstanding musician and rhetorician. He left various brilliant monuments [in writing] of his intelligence. Of these, I have been able to locate only the following: a *Life of St. Dunstan,* in one book; and *On Music,* in one book. He composed many delightfully melodious chants and various other writings, which I have not yet seen. Osbern flourished in the times of the emperor St. Henry, in the year of our Lord 1020.[148]

§67. Christian, Monk

Christian, who is also known as Druthmar, was a monk and priest. He came from Aquitaine to France and stayed for a period in the monastery at Corbie. He was learned in the divine writings and possessed knowledge of both the Greek and Latin tongues. He wrote several works that are worthy of respect. Of these, I have read only his great volume *On the Gospel of Matthew.* He wrote this in clear language, in response to the request of several of his brethren. He is said to have written commentaries on the other Gospels too; but these have not come into my hands.

---

147. Trithemius gives his names as *Osbertus.*

148. Osbern is believed to have lived from about 1050 until about 1090.

§68. Flavaldus, Monk

Flavaldus, a monk of the monastery at Reims, was well educated in the divine writings and magnificently expert in secular literature. He was of penetrating intellect and an effective speaker. He produced a number of works that are well worth reading, and which have passed his name and reputation on to posterity.

Flavaldus wrote the *Deeds of the Bishops of Reims,* presenting an orderly narration from the beginnings of the city. In this work, there is much concerning holy martyrs and other [edifying] matters, which makes it delightful to the studious reader. He wrote also the lives of many saints and the passions of many martyrs, in clear and pleasing language. Flavaldus also produced other works, which have not, however, come to my notice.

§69. Notker, Bishop of Liège

Notker, a German by birth, was the abbot of St. Gall and afterwards the bishop of Liège. Highly learned in the divine scriptures, he also had the reputation for being the leading expert of his time in secular literature. He wrote many brilliant works, in both verse and prose. In these works, the beauty and elegance of his language and the subtlety of his intelligence are well displayed.

Of these, however, only a few have come to my notice. These include a treatise *On Musical Notes and Modes,* in one book; *On the Commentators on Sacred Scriptures,* in one book, to his student Solomon (who later became bishop of Constance); and one book of sequences for use throughout the entire year, which Pope Nicholas [II] confirmed and permitted to be sung in churches. He also produced hymns, songs, poems, letters, sermons, and various tracts. These, however, have not come into my hands.

Notker flourished in the year of our Lord 970.[149]

---

149. Notker is believed to have lived from around 940 to 1008.

§70. Constantine,[150] Monk

Constantine, a monk of Montecassino, was an extremely knowledgeable man in the various fields of secular learning. He was an accomplished physician and philosopher, and fully proficient in Greek, Latin, and Arabic. To this very day, his works are held in great authority with physicians. He wrote many medical treatises and also translated the writings of others from Greek and Arabic into Latin. These are, I believe, well known to practitioners of the medical arts.

Of all these volumes, I have seen only a few. These include: *On Diets in General,* in five books; *On Diets in Particular,* in three books; and *On Weights,* in one book. Concerning his other works, I cannot recall myself have seen any. In the preface of the book, *On Urine,* which he translated from Arabic, he declared himself to have been a monk of Montecassino. He states this also in many other places [in his writings].

§71. Albert of Gembloux

Albert, a monk of Lobbes who afterwards become bishop of Gembloux, was profoundly learned in the divine writings and conversant also with secular learning. He was a strenuous devotee of the discipline of the monastic rule.

Albert wrote narrations of the lives of many saints in polished language and also composed various delightful hymns in their honor (many of which are used in the divine office). He wrote numerous other works, but these have not come to my attention.

Burchard—the bishop of Worms, who (following the example of Isidore) compiled a *decretum*[151]—was a student of his.[152] Albert flourished in the year of our Lord 1000.[153]

150. This Constantine, who was born in Carthage and became a monk of Montecassino, is generally styled as *Constantinus Africanus.* He served as bishop of Salerno and is believed to have died in 1086.

151. I.e., a collection of decrees.

152. See §73.

153. Albert of Gembloux is believed to have died in 1048.

§72. Bertorius of Montecassino

Bertorius, who served as abbot of Montecassino, studied the divine scriptures diligently and was highly educated also in the secular sciences. He was famous as a physician and philosopher. It is said that he composed many works in which his intelligence and character are abundantly displayed. These include a book of brilliant sermons addressed to his brother monks. He is said also to have written certain treatises on medicine, but these works have not come into my hands.

§73. Burchard, Bishop of Worms

Burchard, a monk of Lobbes who later became the bishop of Worms, was once a student of Albert of Gembloux,[154] when both were at the monastery at Lobbes. He applied himself assiduously to the study of the divine writings and became a great teacher. Following the example of Isidor, he compiled a *decretum*[155] out of the writings of the fathers, in twenty books. He also wrote many letters to various persons and certain other works that I have not seen. Gratian[156] makes mentions of Burchard [in his own *decretum*] in his seventy-third distinction, *In nomine Domini*. Burchard flourished in the year of our Lord 1010.[157]

§74. Guido, Monk

Guido of Arezzo, a monk of the monastery of the Holy Cross in Leufroi,[158] was an eloquent and learned man. He was an outstanding master of music, surpassing all others in this discipline. By means of his system, boys and girls may easily learn melodies

154. See §71.

155. I.e., a collection of decrees.

156. I.e., Gratian, the twelfth-century jurist, known as the Father of Canon Law. See §113.

157. Burchard is believed to have lived from about 950 until 1025.

158. La Croix-Saint-Leufroy, in northern France.

previously unknown to them, which are demonstrated through the voice of a teacher or on any instrument and presented to them through six notes or letters, each of which has its own syllable or name assigned to it. These names [which identify the degrees of the scale] are particular to music. By means of this nomenclature and by gestures of the fingers of the left hand, the upward and downward movements of the melody throughout the entire octave are indicated.

Guido wrote a treatise *On Music,* in one book; *On the Body and Blood of the Lord,* in one book; and certain other volumes, which have not come to my notice. He lived during the reign of the emperor St. Henry[159] and flourished in the year of our Lord 1020.[160]

§75. Odilo of Cluny

Odilo, who served as abbot of Cluny, was a learned and holy man, who was glorified by miracles both during his life and after his death. He is said to have composed many sermons addressed to his monastic brethren, which were read studiously in his own times by those who desired salvation. If he wrote anything else, it has not come to my notice.

Peter Damian wrote his biography, in eloquent style. Odilo died in the year of our Lord 1048, in the first indiction, in the eighty-seventh year of his life and the fifty-sixth year of his abbacy.[161]

§76. Helperic, Monk

Helperic, a monk of the monastery of St. Gall, was a German by birth. He was studious and knowledge in the divine scriptures and of distinguished education in secular literature. He was an accomplished philosopher, musician, astronomer, and mathematician.

159. I.e., Henry II.

160. Guido is believed to have lived from about 991 until after 1033.

161. Odilo of Cluny is believed to have lived from about 962 until 1049.

He said to have written many brilliant works. Of these, I have read only his *On Computation and the Art of Calculation,* a most commendable treatise, in one book; and *On Music,* in one book. I have not yet been able to find any of his other works. Helperic flourished in the year of our Lord 1020.

§77. Berno, Abbot of Reichenau

Berno, the abbot of the monastery at Reichenau, a German by birth, was a learned man and an assiduous guardian of the discipline of the monastic rule. He was an extremely studious interpreter of the sacred scriptures, of profound intelligence, and a skilled speaker. He was held in high esteem during his time, because of his great knowledge.

Berno wrote many volumes, but few of these have come into my possession. These few include: *On Advent,* to Aribo, the archbishop of Mainz, in one book; a *Dialogue on the Sabbath Fast,* in one book; *On the Office of the Mass,* in one book; *On the Four Fasts of the Seasons,* in one book; and *On Music and the Rules of Harmony,* in one book.

He also wrote a book on measurements on the monochord.[162] In this work, he goes beyond the rules of Boethius and Guido, adding one tone to the *hypaton* tetrachord and (contrary to the practice of the ancients) usefully inserting the *synemeticon.*

Berno wrote many other works, but these have not come into our hands. He flourished in the year of our Lord 1020.[163]

§78. Albert,[164] Monk of Metz

Albert, a monk of the monastery at Metz, was learned in both divine and secular literature. He was particular knowledgeable of the

---

162. A single-stringed instrument used for calculating and experimenting with musical intervals.

163. Berno of Reichenau is believed to have lived from about 978 until 1048.

164. This name is also often given as Alpert.

histories of past times. He wrote a brief but useful chronicle for the bishop of Metz, in one book. Albert also wrote some other works, which have not come into our hands.

§79. Adam, Abbot of Perseigne[165]

Adam, an abbot of Perseigne, was studious and erudite in the sacred scriptures and no less venerable in his manner of life than in his knowledge. He composed useful sermons for the edification of his brethren, conveying much useful instruction for monks. He wrote also many letters to various persons. He wrote many other works, but these have not come to my notice.

§80. Guitmund, Bishop

Guitmund, a monk of the monastery La Croix-Saint-Leufroy (as I believe) and afterwards bishop of Aversa, was a learned and eloquent man, of distinguished erudition in both sacred and secular literature. In his time, he was held in great esteem and authority. He wrote three books of dialogues, the interlocutors being his own person and a monk called Roger,[166] *On the Body and Blood of the Lord, Against the Error of Berengar the Deacon.* This work is very worthy of studious reading. He is said to have produced other works, but these have not come into my hands. Guitmund lived under the reign of Henry III and flourished in the year of our Lord 1040.[167]

165. Trithemius gives the name of this monastery in the unusual form of *Persenna.* This is a rare case in which he includes a Cistercian author, which seems likely to have been an oversight or error on his part, as he considered Cistercians to be separate from the mainstream Benedictine tradition. Adam of Perseigne is believed to have died sometime after 1200, which makes his inclusion at this point inconsistent with the approximately chronological ordering of entries.

166. See §81.

167. Guitmund is believed to have died in between 1090 and 1095.

§81. Roger, Monk

This Roger was the monk to whom Guitmund, the bishop of Aversa, wrote his three books *On the Body and Blood of the Lord*.[168] He was a studious and learned man, subtle in intellect and prudent in his speech. For the edification of the faithful, he wrote a *Life of St. Bruno, Archbishop of Cologne*. This St. Bruno was a duke, and the brother of the emperor Otto.[169] [Roger] wrote other works too; but these have not come to my notice. He lived during the reign of Henry III and flourished in the year 1040.

§82. Erhard, Monk

Erhard, a monk of a monastery whose name is not given, was studious and learned in the divine writings. He was mentally acute, skillful in his speech, and most expert in the composition and delivery of homilies. He wrote very notable commentaries upon Genesis, Exodus, Leviticus, Numbers, and Deuteronomy, as well as many homilies on the Gospel readings for the liturgical seasons. He also produced commentaries on many other books of the Bible and diverse other tracts, which have not come into my possession.

§83. Smaragdus, Abbot

Smaragdus, an abbot of the monastery of Saint-Mihiel,[170] was extremely studious and learned in the divine scriptures. He was of ready intelligence, a renowned speaker, and worthy of veneration no less for his uprightness of conduct and diligent observance of the monastic rule than for his scholarship. He wrote many brilliant volumes.

Smaragdus expounded the *Ars major* of Donatus[171] in a most beautiful commentary and explicated many questions pertaining

168. See §80.

169. I.e., Otto I.

170. Near Verdun, in northeast France.

171. A famous textbook on Latin grammar.

to secular literature. He wrote a commentary *On the Psalter*, in one book; *On the Four Gospels,* in four books; expositions of the epistle and Gospel readings throughout the entire cycle of the year; *On the Rule of St. Benedict,* in one book; and *On the Epistles of Paul,* in fourteen books. He compiled a collection of readings on the virtues and vices entitled the *Crown of Monks*, which is well worth reading, in one book. He composed many other works also, but these have not come into my hands.

§84. Herman, Monk

Herman, a monk known by the nickname *Contractus*,[172] was a German by nationality and (so it is said) the son [and heir] of the count of Veringenstad. He was a learned man, extremely expert in all secular literature, and most celebrated as a philosopher, astronomer, musician, and poet. In intellect, he was extremely subtle, and in speech, remarkably eloquent. He was also a master of the Greek and Arabic tongues.

Herman composed a great many volumes. Of these, I have read the following: *On Music,* in one book; *On the Six Ages [of the World]*, in one book; *On the Structure of the Astrolabe,* in three books; *On the Usefulness of the Astrolabe,* in one book; *On Eclipses of the Sun and Moon,* in one book; *On Computation* (following [the treatise on the same subject by] Helperic[173]), in one book; and *On Squaring the Circle,* in one book. He wrote the histories and legends of many saints, and composed hymns, antiphons, and delightful chants. Several of these we may still hear sung in our churches. It was this Herman who composed the *Salve regina,* that devout antiphon in praise of the blessed Mary, the mother of God, which the entire church now sings in her honor. He wrote many other works in both verse and prose, which have not come into our hands. He also translated various works from Greek and Arabic into Latin. Copies of these translations are possessed by many.

172. Often rendered in English as "the lame."

173. See §76.

This Herman was (as we have said) the count of Veringenstad in Swabia. In his youth, he became lame, and it was from this affliction that he was given his nickname [*Contractus*]. Once he had become a monk, with great devotion and fervent prayers he implored the Blessed Virgin that she should deign to heal him, through her merits. He is said to have received from her this response: "My dearest son, I have heard your diligent prayers, and have procured for you the option of two choices. Choose which you prefer! Either you may remain lame but receive knowledge of all writings; or you may receive physical healing, but you shall remain a simpleton.[174] If you choose this second option, you will also become a bishop.[175] Now, which of these two options would you prefer?"

Herman carefully considered the options that the Queen of Heaven had proposed to him. And he chose to remain lame but to receive knowledge of all sacred lore, rather than to possess physical soundness without learning. Now, at that time he was still totally uneducated and knew no languages except for the vernacular[176] but was highly devout and inflamed with an ardent love of scripture.

From that time forth, he began to excel beyond all his contemporaries in knowledge of the sacred writings and soon became a man of the highest reputation. He mastered three languages— Latin, Greek, and Arabic—with such proficiency as if he had been born into their use. I myself have seen many books of Aristotle and other ancient authors that Herman translated from Arabic into Latin. These include Aristotle's treatises on rhetoric and poetry, his works on astronomy (as far they are relevant to ecclesiastical computations), and also various other writings.

Hermanus flourished in the year of our Lord 1060.[177]

174. Latin: *idiota*.

175. This apparently incongruous *addendum* to the second option (whereby Herman would remain an *idiota* but became a bishop) may be intended to be read with a certain degree of humorous irony.

176. Latin: *idiota*.

177. Herman is believed to have lived from 1013 until 1054.

§85. Bruno, Archbishop and Martyr

Bruno was a monk of a certain monastery in Italy (the name of which does not occur to me), who later became archbishop of the Ruthenians. He was a learned and holy man and an outstanding preacher of the word of God. He wrote a brilliant work on Genesis and certain other items, which have not come into my hands. After many labors preaching the word of God, Bruno was crowned with holy martyrdom for his faith in Christ, at the hands of the Prussians, in the year of our Lord 1008, in the sixth indication.[178]

§86. Theodoric, Monk

Theodoric, a monk of Hersfeld monastery, was a German by birth. A learned and eloquent man, he was mentally astute and extremely well read in the divine writings. He wrote the *Life and Praises of St. Benedict,* to Richard, the abbot of Fulda, in one book; the *Translation of St. Benedict to Fleury,* in one book; and *On the Places in the Holy Land,* in one book. He produced other works as well, which I have not had the good fortune to see.[179] Theodoric flourished in the year of our Lord 1030.[180]

§87. Alfanus, Archbishop

Alfanus was a monk of Montecassino, who went on to become archbishop of Salerno. He was a highly celebrated philosopher and orator in his time and magnificently learned in sacred literature. We wrote a number of profound works, displaying his great intelligence. Of these, the following survive: *On the Four Humors of the Human Body,* in one book; *On the Union of the Body and Soul,* in

---

178. St. Bruno of Querfurt (to whom Trithemius is clearly referring here) is believed to have lived from about 947 until his martyrdom in 1009.

179. Latin: *videre non merui.*

180. Theodoric (sometimes styled as Diederic) of Hersfeld is believed to have lived from 950 to 1027.

one book; *On the Union of the Word and the Flesh,* in one book. I have not been able to discover the other works he wrote.[181]

§88. Anselm, Monk

Anselm, a monk of Reims, was learned in the divine scriptures and well instructed also in the humanities. He was sharp in his intellect and renowned for his eloquence. He is said to have composed numerous works, in which his ingenuity is magnificently displayed. Out of these, I have been able to find only his relation of the journey of Pope Leo IX from Rome to France. In this work, he describes the deeds [of Leo IX] at the synod at Reims and at other places, as he examined ecclesiastical matters with justice and authority. He shows how [Leo IX] corrected sinners with firmness and how divine virtue worked through him. This was demonstrated particularly well in the case of the bishop of Freising—who, when he contumaciously resisted the apostolic authority of the holy pontiff, was suddenly rendered mute in the sight of all!

[Anselm of Reims] wrote other works beyond this, which have not come to my notice. He flourished in the year of our Lord 1050.[182]

§89. Humbert, Cardinal

Humbert, a monk of Toul in the region of Lorraine, was a man of incomparable learning, outstandingly expert in his knowledge of both divine and secular literature. Nevertheless, he was no less venerable for his sanctity than for his scholarship. On account of the excellence of his learning, Pope Leo IX took him from Lorraine with himself [when he was sent to Rome to take up the papal office]. He then sent him to preach the word of God in Siculis,[183] ordaining him first as archbishop [of that place] and, subsequently,

181. St. Alfanus I became archbishop of Salerno in 1058. He lived from about 1015 or 1020 until 1085.

182. Anselm of Reims is believed to have died in 1056.

183. A city in Catania.

as a cardinal in Rome. Leo next assigned Humbert to a mission of refuting heretics in Constantinople, where he successfully overcome [another] Leo, the bishop of the Bulgarians. Humbert [also] refuted Nicetas Pictoratus, a [heterodox] monk, so effectively that he was compelled to renounce and burn his books with his own hands in the presence of the emperor Constantine.[184] Humbert wrote down all that he said in this matter, in the form of a dialogue between a Roman and a Constantinopolitan. He wrote other works as well, but these have not come to my notice. Humbert flourished in the year of our Lord 1050.[185]

§90. Alger, Monk

Alger was a scholar who became a monk of the monastery at Corvey in Saxony. He was of German nationality, very learned in the divine scriptures, and a most expert teacher of secular literature. His character was astute but ardent. Alger wrote a great volume entitled *On the Sacrament of the Altar,* in three books; and *On Grace and Free Will,* in one book. He also wrote many other works, which have not come into our hands.[186]

§91. Bernard, Monk

Bernard, a monk of Cluny, was a studious lover of the divine scriptures and an expert interpreter of secular literature. He wrote a customary[187] of the monastery at Cluny, at the behest of Hugh, his abbot. This work proved most useful in the preservation of the discipline of the monastic rule. He is said to have written various other works, which have not come into our hands.

184. I.e., Constantine IX.

185. Cardinal Humbert (known as Humbert of Silva Candida) is believed to have died in 1061.

186. The writings mentioned by Trithemius indicate that the person referred to here is the same as Alger of Liège (1055–1131). Other sources describe him as a monk of Cluny.

187. I.e., a compilation of the customs and practices of a particular monastery.

Bernard of Cluny flourished in the year of our Lord 1050.[188]

§92. Arnulf, Monk

Arnulf, a monk, was studious and knowledgeable in the divine scriptures and of singular devotion to the cultivation of learning.[189] He was renowned for his intelligence and abilities as a speaker and excelled in the composition of both poetry and prose. He is said to have written many works. These include a great work on the Proverbs of Solomon, written in verse, in one book. Of his other writings, I have not been able to find anything.[190]

§93. Peter Damian, Bishop

Peter Damian was monk at the monastery in Viviers,[191] who later became bishop of Ostia and a cardinal. He was a most erudite man in the divine scriptures, penetrating in his intelligence and skillful in his speech. Indeed, he was the very image of Gregory [the Great] in the persuasiveness of his beautiful and delightful eloquence.

He exerted himself strenuously for some years in his episcopate in governing his diocese and in correcting (without deference to persons) the vices of the wicked. After this, feeling the effects of old age and fatigue, he left the episcopate in order to attend more diligently to his own salvation. By returning to a monastic life [after his service as a bishop], he followed the examples of Gregory the

188. Although the dates of Bernard of Cluny are not known with certainty, he is believed to have lived in the twelfth century. The eleventh-century Cluniac customary, written at the request of Hugh, is attributed to Uldaric of Cluny.

189. There is a certain playful treatment of words in the Latin text, which has not been reproduced in the translation given above. Arnulf is described as a *singularis doctrinae cultor singularis* (literally, "a singular cultivator of a singular learning").

190. The mention of a work in verse on the Proverbs of Solomon suggests that the person referred to here is the same as Ernulf (or Arnulf), a French monk who became archbishop of Rochester and to whom such a work is attributed. Ernulf of Rochester is believed to have lived from 1040 until 1124.

191. In southern France.

Great and Gregory Nazianzus. However, no less than three Roman pontiffs expressed disappointment that a man of such learning and usefulness to the church should desert the episcopate and give priority to his own needs over those of the community, particularly as he was so well suited (both in his words and his example) for the governance of the souls of others.

But Peter humbly excused himself, writing apologetic tracts explaining his resolution to withdraw from the episcopal office. By means of the sound reasons and examples he provided in these, he successfully reconciled the pontiffs to his decision.

He also wrote many other volumes. Of [Peter Damian's works], I have found the following: his *Apologia* to Pope Nicholas II, in one book; his *Apologia* to Popes Alexander II and Gregory VII, in two books; *On the Progress of Monks*, in one book; *Antilogion against the Jews*, in one book; *On the Avarice of Prelates*, in one book; *Against Simoniac Bishops*, in one book; *On the Celibacy of Priests*, in one book; *On the Wives of Clergy*, in one book; a treatise addressed to Leo the Hermit (on the question of whether a hermit, when praying, should say "The Lord be with you," even though there is no one present to respond), in one book; a *Rule for Hermits and Anchorites*, in one book; and an *Exhortation to the Brethren*, in one book; *On Certain Astonishing Events Occurring in his Times*, in one book; a *Life of St. Odilo, Abbot of Cluny*, in one book; *On the Terror of Death*, in one book; a *Meditation on Death*, in one book; and [*The Passion of Saints*] *Flora and Lucilla*, in one book; another work that is known as the *Liber Gratissimus* (or *Probatissimus*),[192] in one book; a tract against a certain bishop who called monks back to the world, in one book; *On the Insolence of Wicked Persons*, in one book; a tract [*Against*] *Rhetorical Declamations*, in one book; *On the Nature of Certain Animals*, in one book; *On St. Cassian, Martyr*, in one book; *On St. Boniface*, in one book; and *On the Site and Foundation of the Monastery at Viviers*, in one book.

Peter Damian wrote virtually innumerable sermons and homilies, which are of distinguished eloquence. He also wrote numerous letters to various persons and many other works, which

---

192. "Most pleasing [or most approved] book."

have not come into our hands. He lived during the reign of Henry III and flourished in year of our Lord 1060.[193]

§94. Gunther, Monk

Gunther, a monk of the monastery of St. Amand, was learned in the divine scriptures, well informed concerning secular literature, and an accomplished theologian and poet. He wrote the *Passion of St. Cyriac, Martyr,* in one book. Gunther is said to have written many other works, of both poetry and prose. These, however, have not come into our hands.[194]

§95. Marianus Scotus

Marianus Scotus, a monk of the monastery at Fulda, came to Germany [from Ireland] as a pilgrim, inspired by the love of Christ. He first became a monk at the monastery of St. Pantaleon in Cologne and remained there for some two years, living an enclosed life.[195] After this he departed from Cologne and went to the monastery at Fulda, where remained for eleven years, living in enclosure. Then, upon the command of his abbot and the archbishop of Mainz, he moved to Mainz, joining the monastery of St. Martin there. He remained enclosed in that place then until the day of his death.

Marianus was held in the highest esteem by all because of the excellence of his doctrine and the sanctity of his life. He wrote a wonderful chronicle, from the beginning of the world until his own times. With amazing astuteness, he revealed the error made by earlier chronographers who placed the years of the birth and passion of Christ in a way that did not properly accord with the truth of the gospel. He himself placed the year of Christ's birth

---

193. Peter Damian is believed to have lived from about 1007 until 1072 or 1073.

194. In *De Scriptoribus Ecclesiasticis,* it is stated that Gunther flourished in the year 1100. Trithemius, *De Scriptoribus Ecclesiasticis,* 80.

195. The term *inclusus* is used here to describe Marianus, suggesting an anchoritic mode of life. But it is also possible that it indicates the observance regular monastic enclosure.

twenty-three years prior to the year usually assigned to it by earlier chronographers, giving in his work (in parallel columns) the years matching the truth of the gospel, as well as the years of the incorrect, prior calculations. In this way, the reader is able to discern the distinction between the true and false chronologies not only mentally but also visually.

He also wrote *On the Concordance of the Gospels,* in one book; and certain other works that remain unknown to us. His chronicle extends to the year of our Lord 1082. Marianus Scotus died in 1086, in the ninth indication, in the fifty-eighth year of his life. His was entombed at Mainz at the monastery of St. Martin, with great honor.[196]

§96. Theodoric, Abbot

Theodoric, the abbot of the monastery St. Trudo in the diocese of Liège, was well versed in the divine writings and of distinguished learning in secular literature. Excelling in both poetry and prose, he was particularly studious in writing the deeds of the saints. He composed in verse a *Life of St. Trudo,* in one book; a *Life of St. Bavo,* in one book; and a *Life of St. Reinold,* in one book. He is said to have produced many other writings, but these have not come into my hands.[197]

§97. Williram of Ebersberg

Williram, the abbot of Ebersberg, was a German by birth. First, he was a scholar at the church at Bamberg. Later, renouncing the world, he became a monk at Fulda, and finally abbot at the aforesaid monastery at Ebersberg. He was a most learned man and perfectly instructed in both the divine scriptures and secular literature. He excelled in both poetry and prose, writing numerous

196. Marianus Scotus is believed to have lived from 1028 until 1082 or 1083.

197. In *De Scriptoribus Ecclesiasticis,* it is stated that Theodoric flourished in the year 1100. Trithemius, *De Scriptoribus Ecclesiasticis,* 80.

works that are well worth reading. Of these, however, I have seen only his *Exposition of the Songs of Songs* on the marriage of Christ with the church, written in verse, in three books. The other works that he wrote have not come to me. Williram flourished in the year of our Lord 1070.

§98. Luke, Abbot

Luke, abbot of the monastery of Mount St. Cornelius, was scholarly and learned in the divine scriptures and knowledgeable also in secular literature. His is said to have produced various works that are worth reading. Of these, I have been able to find only his great work *On the Song of Songs,* to Milo, bishop of Thérouanne. Of the other works that he is said to have written, I have discovered nothing.[198]

§99. Lanfranc, Archbishop

Lanfranc was abbot of the monastery at Caen[199] before becoming archbishop of Canterbury. He was a most learned man in the divine writings and held in high esteem by all for his expertise in secular literature. He was regarded as the leading figure in dialectics in his time and was esteemed as a beacon and master for theologians.

Born in the Italian city of Pavia, he devoted himself to long study of literature and for many years conducted a public academy with illustrious distinction. For the purpose of furthering his studies, he crossed the Alps and made his way towards Normandy. While on his journey to Rouen, bandits set upon him. He was abducted and robbed by these, who left him, under the dark cover of night, in an out-of-the-way forest. Lanfranc bemoaned his fate for a while but then fell to reflection. He said to himself, "Woe is me! For so long I have devoted myself to literary studies, but never have I learned how to praise God while in the midst of tribulation."

198. In *De Scriptoribus Ecclesiasticis,* it is stated that Luke flourished in the year 1130. Trithemius, *De Scriptoribus Ecclesiasticis,* 84.

199. In Normandy.

Lanfranc then earnestly vowed himself to the service of God. Once he was freed from these perils, he entered the monastery at Bec and made his monastic profession under the abbot Herluin.

For three years, he remained unknown in the monastery, rejoicing that he dwelt in humble obscurity in the house of the Lord. But at last his identity was made known [to the other monks] by some merchants from Italy.

[But long before this happened,] on a certain day, he was reading at the table. And he happened to read a particular word, using the correct pronunciation in an exemplary fashion. But the prior, who was not highly educated, corrected him for this pronunciation [which seemed to him to be erroneous] and instructed him to say it otherwise, as if he were teaching him. Lanfranc rejoiced to be thus humiliated for the love of God. Knowing that obedience to Christ [in the person of his monastic superior] was of more value than obedience to Donatus,[200] he then ceased using the correct pronunciation and began saying the word in the manner in which the prior had directed (even though he knew this to be wrong).

Then for the next three years, during which his learning remained unknown, he conducted himself with such humility as if he had never undertaken literary studies at all. And thus he never read anything before the community unless he read it first privately to the master of novices [to check his pronunciation and delivery].

But once it became known who he really was [and the extent of his learning], he was appointed prior of his monastery and directed to conduct a public school. After this, he became abbot of the monastery at Caen. Finally, he was appointed as archbishop of Canterbury, strenuously governing the church entrusted to him both by his doctrine and [the example of] his holy life.

He wrote numerous works of great authority. Of these, I have found the following: *Commentaries on all the Epistles of Paul,* which he presents, wherever opportune, in the style of dialogues; *Against Berengar, Cleric of Tours and Deacon of Angers, on the Body and Blood of the Lord,* an outstanding work, in one book; and the *Deeds of William, the Duke of Normandy* (who first invaded the

---

200. The author of an authoritative textbook on grammar.

kingdom of England), in one book. He wrote various other works, which have not come into our hands.

Lanfranc flourished in the year of our Lord 1060.[201]

§100. Engelbert, Abbot

Engelbert, abbot of the monastery at Admont, was industrious in the reading of divine writings and also adequately instructed (for one of his position) in secular literature. He was renowned for his intelligence and eloquence, and venerable no less for his conduct of life than for his knowledge. He wrote elegant sermons for the edification of his brethren, in which he clearly explained the scriptures to the extent that he was able. He wrote also a treatise *On the Vices and Virtues,* in one book; and certain other works, which remain to us unknown.

§101. Anselm of Canterbury

Anselm was the abbot of Bec monastery, when he succeeded Lanfranc as archbishop of Canterbury. Anselm had been a student of Lanfranc[202] and had succeeded him as prior and rector of the monastery school at Bec. He was a holy man and deeply learned in both divine and secular literature.

When he served as abbot, in order to encourage his brethren in their studies of the sacred writings, he permitted all the monks to ask him any questions that occurred to them with the most perfect freedom. And he said that they should never cease from asking questions, until they were completely satisfied with the response they had received. He did this so that the occasion and material for learning and inquiry should never be lacking, either to himself or to the brethren.

Anselm wrote a great many very brilliant works. Of these, I have been able to find the following: *Why God [Became] Man,*

201. Lanfranc is believed to have been born sometime between 1005 and 1010, and to have died in 1089.

202. See §99.

in two books; *Against the Jews, on the Incarnation of the Word*, in one book; *On the Virginal Conception*, addressed to Boso, in one book; the *Monologion*, in one book; the *Proslogion*, in one book; the *Proceeding of the Holy Spirit, Against the Greeks*, in one book; the *Fall of the Devil*, in one book; *On the Diversity of the Sacraments*, in one book; *On Yeast and Unleavened Bread*, in one book; *On the Will of God*, in one book; *On the Compatibility of the Grace of God and Human Free Will*, in one book; *On Free Will*, in one book; *On Truth*, in one book; *On Similitudes*, in one book; *On the Measure of the Cross*, in one book; *Meditations or Prayers*, in one book; *Meditations on Human Redemption*, in one book; *On the Passion of the Lord*, in one book; *Against the Fool*, in one book; *For the Fool*, in one book;[203] *On the Misery of Humankind*, in one book; *On the [Bodily] Members That Are Attributed to God in the Scriptures*, in one book; *On the Sacraments and Divine Offices*, in two books; *On the House of Conscience*, in one book; *On the Holy Trinity*, in one book; *On the Song of Songs*, in one book; *On Peace and Concord*, in one book; *On Blessed Sufficiency*, in one book; *On the Blessed Life*, in one book; *On Good Occupations*, in one book; *In Praise of Holy Mary*, in one book; *The Antichrist*, in one book; a *Dialogue between a Christian and a Pagan*, in one book; *On the Beatitudes*, in one book; *On Celestial Beatitude*, in one book; *To Bishop Lanfranc*, in one book; *On the Hexameron*, in one book; and *On Grammar*, in one book.

Anselm also wrote various sermons and homilies, and many letters to diverse persons. Out of these, I have found one to Wilhelm, who was the abbot of the monastery at Hirsau and a very brilliant man.[204] Anselm had a special affection for this Wilhelm, as his letter to him testifies. He also wrote a number of other works, which have not come into our hands.

Anselm flourished in the year of our Lord 1080.[205]

---

203. This book and the previous one offer real or hypothetical objections to the arguments advanced in the *Proslogion* and responses to these.

204. See §102.

205. Anselm of Canterbury is believed to have lived from about 1033 until 1109.

§102. Wilhelm of Hirsau

Wilhelm served as the abbot of the monastery at Hirsau,[206] within the borders of the Swabia, in the diocese of Speyer. He was a special friend of blessed Anselm, archbishop of Canterbury. Well versed in the divine scriptures and nobly instructed in secular learning, he was no less venerable for his virtue than for his knowledge. Indeed, it is written that while he was still living the flesh he shone forth with many miracles. [For example,] once when he was passing over the bridge approaching the monastery of St. Aurelius,[207] he encountered a certain lame man on the way. Wilhelm poured out prayers to God, and the man was instantly healed.

He wrote various works that deserve reading. Of these, I have seen the following: *On Music,* in one book; *On Horology,* in one book; and his *Constitutions* (for the monastic reformation that took place, through his efforts, both in his own monastery and many others), in two books. He also made corrections to the psalter and wrote many letters to various persons. [But] these letters are rarely to be found collected together.

He had previously been a monk of the monastery of St. Emmeram in Regensburg, when, with unanimous consent, he was elected as abbot at Hirsau. He served in that role for some twenty years. He died in on June 3, in the year of our Lord 1091, in the fourteenth indication, under the reign of Henry IV.[208]

§103. Peregrinus [or Conrad],[209] Monk

Peregrinus was a monk at [the monastery at] Hirsau and a one-time student of Wilhelm, the abbot of that monastery. He was most learned in both divine and secular writings, of keen intellect, and

---

206. In southwest Germany.

207. I.e., Wilhelm's monastery at Hirsau,

208. Wilhelm is believed to have lived from about 1030 to 1091.

209. In *De Scriptoribus Ecclesiasticis,* the name of this author is given as Conrad (by which he is more commonly known), with Peregrinus being noted as the name under which he wrote his works. Trithemius, *De Scriptoribus Ecclesiasticis,* 87.

succinct, skillful, and brilliant in his expression. As an orator and poet, he was inferior to none of his predecessors. He wrote certain outstanding works in both verse and prose. Of these, I have seen the following: a large and significant volume in beautiful language, written under the persons of himself and a certain Theodora, a virgin of Christ, whose title is the *Mirror of Virgins,* in eight books; a commentary on the gospel, in one book; *On the Life of the Spirit and the Fruit of Death,* in one book; the *Dialogue of a Matricularius,*[210] in one book; and his *Didascolon,* in two books. He also composed, in verse, a poem entitled *In Praise of St. Benedict.*

All of his works, which are characterized by [smoothly] flowing language, are written in the form of dialogues. Peregrinus flourished in the year of our Lord 1100.[211]

§104. Franco, Abbot

Franco, an abbot of the monastery at Hasslingen, was studious and learned in the divine writings and by no means ignorant of secular learning. While he was still a monk, at the command and insistence of his abbot, Fulgentius, he commenced writing his great work, *On the Grace of God.* Franco completed this work after he himself had become abbot, following the death of Fulgentius. He wrote an elegant work in verse, *On the State of Future Glory.* He is said also to have written other works, but these have not come into my hands.[212]

§105. Giselbert of Westminster

Giselbert, the prior of the monastery of Westminster in England, had once been a student of blessed Anselm of Canterbury. He

---

210. I.e., A clerical officer in charge of taking registrations of students.

211. In *De Scriptoribus Ecclesiasticis,* Trithemius states that Conrad (alias Peregrinus) flourished in the year 1150. Trithemius, *De Scriptoribus Ecclesiasticis,* 87. He is believed to have lived from about 1070 to about 1150.

212. In *De Scriptoribus Ecclesiasticis,* Trithemius states that Franco flourished in the year 1060. Trithemius, *De Scriptoribus Ecclesiasticis,* 78.

was a scholarly and learned man, of ready intellect and prudent speech. His works include: *A Dispute between a Christian and a Jew on the Christian Faith,* dedicated to Anselm; *On the Prophet Isaiah,* in one book; *On the Song of Songs,* in one book. He wrote also many other works, which remain unknown to me. Giselbert flourished in the year of our Lord 1100.[213]

§106. Ansbert, Monk

Ansbert (also known as Ambrose),[214] a monk, was highly studious and learned in the divine scriptures and also well educated in secular literature. He was of ready understanding and a renowned speaker. He wrote many brilliant works, but only a few of them have come to me. These include: *On the Song of Songs,* in one book; *On the Psalter,* in one book; *On the Apocalypse of John,* in ten books; and *On Cupidity* [or *Desire*], in one book. He also wrote letters to diverse persons, and various sermons.

Ansbert flourished in the year of our Lord 1180. However, there are others who assert that he flourished in the year of our Lord 890. And perhaps these judge the matter more correctly . . .[215]

§107. Ekkehard, Abbot

Ekkehard, a German by nationality, was the first abbot of the monastery of St. Laurence the Martyr, in Aura in Würzburg. He was learned in both divine and secular writings, and a distinguished theologian, orator, and poet, no less admirable for his [sanctity of] life than for his knowledge. He produced a work on the consolations of monks, in imitation of Boethius,[216] mixing both genres of

213. Giselbert of Westminster (known as Giselbert Crispinus) is believed to have lived from 1084 until 1117.

214. In *De Scriptoribus Ecclesiasticis,* Trithemius identifies this writer only as Ambrose (*Ambrosius*), but the name Ansbert is also given in the index. Trithemius, *De Scriptoribus Ecclesiasticis,* 68.

215. In *De Scriptoribus Ecclesiasticis,* Trithemius gives the year 890, rather than 1180. Trithemius, *De Scriptoribus Ecclesiasticis,* 68.

216. That is, in imitation of Boethius's *The Consolation of Philosophy.*

writing (that is, poetry and prose), in five books. To this work he gave the title *The Lantern of Monks*. If he produced more writings than this, they have not come to my notice. Ekkehard flourished in the year of our Lord 1120.[217]

§108. Honorius, Monk

Honorius was a monk in England who, for the love of Christ, lived an enclosed life. He was a close friend of blessed Anselm, archbishop of Canterbury, and a number of Honorius's letters to Anselm survive. He was a learned and devout man, who wrote a number of pious works. These include his *Diverse Questions and Responses,* in one book. He also composed certain letters, which are useful for inspiring compunction. Honorius flourished in the times of Anselm, in the year 1080.[218]

§109. Rupert of Deutz

Rupert, a German by birth, served as the abbot of the monastery at Deutz, near the city of Cologne. He was learned in the sacred scriptures, through the inspiration of the Holy Spirit, and no less renowned for his conduct of life than for his doctrine. For while he still did not know any languages and was therefore unable to understand the holy writings, he prayed to Blessed Mary, the mother of God. With devout and earnest entreaties, he implored that she should obtain for him understanding and knowledge of the scriptures from her Son, who is himself the font of all wisdom. Then the Blessed Virgin appeared to him in a vision, saying: "I

217. Ekkehard is believed to have died in 1126.

218. It seems possible that Trithemius is here speaking of Honorius Augustodunensis, who is known to have travelled to England and studied and corresponded with Anselm, and who does not receive a separate entry in the present work. Honorius Augustodunensis is believed to have lived from about 1080 until about 1140. Honorious Augustodunensis is the only writer by the name of Honorius given an entry in *De Scriptoribus Ecclesiasticis,* where a much more extensive listing of his works is provided. See Trithemius, *De Scriptoribus Ecclesiasticis,* 80–81.

have heard your prayers, my child, and will obtain for you that which you have so earnestly requested. Behold, all the secrets of scripture shall be opened to you, such that there will be no one who is your equal among your contemporaries! Take comfort and be strong, for your efforts will prove useful to many. But take care that you do not languish in idleness, lest the grace that has been bestowed upon you shall pass you by and lest the talent that has been entrusted to you should be buried in the earth, through vain desire for the things of this passing world!"

In a certain place [in his writings], Rupert confessed also that various other secrets were revealed to him [in this vision], but these he would never dare to disclose to anyone. From that time until his death, he understood and expounded the sacred scriptures with such love and holy desire that he would never cease from studying them, even for a moment. Always did he read, pray, or write, not even sparing from these effort the hours of the night (as other are accustomed to do).

In order that he could devote himself to this pursuit with greater liberty, he committed the care of the temporal matters [of the monastery] to others who were suitable for such responsibilities and applied himself intently to his internal studies. And he wrote many brilliant volumes. He himself provides a listing of his works in one of his letters, as shown below: *On the Divine Offices,* in twelve books; a *Commentary on Job,* in ten books; *On the Gospel of John,* in fourteen books; *On the Works of the Holy and Undivided Trinity,* in forty books; *On the Apocalypse of John,* in twelve books; *On the Twelve Minor Prophets,* in ten books; *On the Victory of the Word of God,* to Cuno, abbot of Sigenberg and afterwards archbishop of Regensburg, in thirteen books; *On the Gospel of Matthew,* to the same [Cuno], in eight books; *On the Books of the Kings, about the Glorious David,* to Frederick archbishop of Cologne, in eleven books; *On the Song of Songs,* in seven books; *On the Rule of our Holy Father Benedict,* in four books; an *Apologia* for his own works, in one book; *On the Fire at the Monastery at Deutz,* written in imitation of the *Confessions* of Augustine (a work well adapted to devotion), in three books. He is said also to have written commentaries on the four Gospels and many other books of the Bible, but these have not come into our hands.

Rupert of Deutz flourished under the reign of Henry V, in the year of our Lord 1120. He died during the reign of Lothair III.[219]

§110. Rupert, Monk

Rupert, abbot of Limburg Abbey in the diocese of Speyer, was a German by birth and venerable for the rectitude of his conduct and his careful observance of the monastic rule. He was erudite and studious in the divine scriptures and well educated also in secular literature. Before his conversion [to monastic life] he had devoted many years to the study of secular philosophy at the University of Paris and had acquired there considerable reputation and learning. But at last, reflecting upon the inconstancy of this present life, he returned to his native land. Dedicating himself entirely to God, he became a monk at the aforesaid monastery [of Limburg], where, with ever increasing merits, he was [in due course] elected as abbot, with the unanimous support of the community.

Rupert was of such purity and devotion that he merited to be refreshed and illuminated by many divine revelations. Inspired by a vision, he composed a commentary *On the Song of Songs*, in four books. [He also wrote] *On the Contempt of the World and the Love of God*, in two books; and one book containing some of his own revelations. He wrote also a number of praiseworthy sermons on the saints whose relics are kept at Limburg Abbey or who are venerated as patrons of that monastery.

Rupert of Limburg flourished in the year of our Lord 1124.

§111. Bernard, Monk

Bernard, a German by birth and a monk of Corvey in Saxony, was well instructed in the divine scriptures and excellently educated in secular literature. He wrote to Hartuvinus, the archbishop of

219. Rupert of Deutz is believed to have lived from about 1075 until about 1129.

Magdeburg, a brilliantly expressed but bitter tract, in one book, *Against the Emperor Henry IV*, who was a rebel against Pope Gregory VII. He is said to have written many other works, but these have not come into our hands. He flourished in the times of Henry IV, in the year of our Lord 1100.

§112. Sigebert, Monk

Sigebert, a monk of the monastery at Gembloux, was most learned in the sacred writings and also highly expert in secular literature. He was of keen intellect and an accomplished speaker. His teaching was held in great authority during his own times, as is clearly exhibited in his works, which he wrote for various princes and prelates of churches. In a certain place [in his writings] Sigebert himself compiled a list of his own writings,[220] which is given below: *Histories* or *Chronicle of His Times*, a great and significant volume; *On Illustrious Persons*, in one book; a *Life of St. Theodoric, Bishop of Metz*, written in heroic meter, in one book; a *Life of King Sigebert*, in one book; the *Passion of St. Lucia, Martyr*, in elegiac verse, in one book; *On the Translation of the Body of* [*St. Lucia*] *to Metz*, in one book; the *Passion of the Holy Martyrs of Thebes*, in heroic meter, in one book; the *Life of St. Guibert, Monk and Founder of Gembloux Monastery*, in one book; the *Deeds of the Abbots of Gembloux*, in one book; and a tract *Against Those Who Have Calumniated* [*the Validity of*] *the Masses of Married Priests*, addressed to the emperor Henry IV, in one book. At the request of the same [Emperor Henry IV], he wrote to the [clergy] of Trier *On the Fasts of the Four Seasons*, in one book. [He composed also a] *Threefold Exposition of Ecclesiastes*, in heroic verse, in one book.

Sigebert wrote many letters to diverse persons and various sermons and tracts, [the details of] which have not come to my notice. He revised the biographies of various [saints], presenting them in a more polished style. He also composed responsories,

220. In *De Scriptoribus Ecclesiasticis*, Trithemius identifies this catalogue of writings as being found at the end of Sigebert's *De Viris Illustribus*. Trithemius, *De Scriptoribus Ecclesiasticis*, 81.

hymns, and antiphons in praise of the saints, setting them to delightful melodies.

Sigebert commenced his monastic life at the monastery at Gembloux but was later transferred to the monastery at Metz, for the purpose of instructing the junior brethren there in fundamental studies. [While at Metz,] he produced some writings in praise of that city. After his time there, he returned to his monastery in Gembloux. All the time of his life he devoted to the study of writings, and he earned for himself great praise for his learning and teaching. He flourished under the reign of the emperor Henry IV, in the year of our Lord 1120.[221]

§113. Gratian, Monk

Gratian, a monk of [either] Bologna or Classe, was highly studious in the divine writings and rich also in his knowledge of the ancient authors, being well instructed in secular literature. According to the example of Ruth the Moabite, he followed the harvesters and carefully gleaned the remaining crops behind them.[222] In this way, he became a great man, diligently seeking out the opinions of the church fathers and the rulings of councils. It was thus that he compiled that most noble work, his *decretum* (which he entitled *A Concord of Discordant Canons*[223]), in four books. He is said to have written other works as well, but these have not come into our hands.

Regarding the variety of decretals in existence, it is to be noted that Isidor, bishop of Seville, compiled a decretal of great magnitude, from the judgments of the fathers and church councils, in the year of our Lord 530. After this, Burchard, bishop of Worms (of whom we have made mention above), compiled a decretal in some twenty books,[224] in the year of our Lord 1023. After him,

---

221. Sigebert of Glemboux is believed to have lived from around 1030 until 1112.

222. See Ruth 2:2–3.

223. Latin: *Concordia discordantium canonum.*

224. See §73.

Ivo, bishop of Chartres, abridged the collection of decrees into ten books, in the year of our Lord 1095.

Finally, this Gratian (of whom we speak), observing that the material was all dispersed without proper order in the various decretals of the aforementioned earlier writers, applied his own hand to the task. With diligent effort, he composed [his own decretal] in the year of our Lord 1127. And this compilation of decrees is still used by the church until the present day.

There have been many others who have made compilations of decrees, drawing upon the judgments of the church fathers and councils. These include Ansegisus, abbot of Lobbes;[225] and Regino of Prüm;[226] and numerous others. But these have not been universal [in their scope], nor have they became so widely used in the church of God [as that of Gratian].

Gratian flourished in the year of our Lord 1130.[227]

§114. Eadmer,[228] Monk

Eadmer, a monk of Canterbury, was a studious and learned man. He is said to have left a number of [literary] memorials of his intelligence, in which the abundance of his talent in both genres of writings [that is, both poetry and prose,] is to be seen. Out of these, I have been able to find a *Life of St. Anselm of Canterbury,* in one book; *On the Disagreement between King William and Archbishop Anselm*; and *On the Liberty of the Church,* in one book. I have discovered nothing of the other works that he composed. Eadmer flourished during the times of the emperor Henry IV, in the year of our Lord 1120.[229]

225. See §45.

226. See §54.

227. Gratian's years of birth and death remain uncertain, but he is believed to have died around the middle of the twelfth century.

228. Trithemius gives this name as *Emundus.*

229. Eadmer is believed to have lived for around 1060 to around 1126.

§115. Hugh, Monk

Hugh, known by the cognomen "of Fouilloy," was a monk of Corbie in France. He was studious and learned in the divine writings and well instructed in secular literature. Pleasing and clear in his speech, he was distinguished no less for his uprightness of conduct than for his knowledge. Having been taught by his own experience, he wrote several brilliant works for the edification of monks. Of these, I have been able to find the following: *On the Physical Cloister,* in one book; *On the Spiritual Cloister,* in one book; *On the Cloister of the Soul,* in one book; *On the Cloister of Paradise, or the Celestial Cloister,* in one book. I have not seen any other works that he wrote. Hugh flourished in the times of Henry IV, in the year of our Lord 1120.[230]

§116. Adelphus, Abbot

The abbot Adelphus studied the divine scriptures thoroughly and was also by no means ignorant of secular literature. He is said to have written elegant and delightful sermons for the edification of his brethren, copies of which are possessed by many. He also wrote a tract *Against the Errors of the Perfidious Mahomet and the Saracens,* in one book. He is said to have written many other works, which I have not been able to see.

§117. Joachim, Abbot

Joachim served as abbot of the monastery at Fiore in Calabria. He was learned in the divine scriptures and open and direct in his speech. He was, [however,] rightly reprehended for his own attempted refutations of Peter Lombard of Paris, since Joachim dared to disagree with the perfectly correct things which Peter Lombard had said about the Holy Trinity. And for this, Joachim's book [in which he imprudently reprehended Peter Lombard] suffered due and deserved censure.

---

230. Hugh of Fouilloy is believed to have died in about 1172.

However, neither Joachim himself nor his other works (beyond *On the Highest Trinity and the Catholic Faith* [in which he refutes the opinions of Peter Lombard on the Holy Trinity]) were condemned [in the decree commencing with the word] *Damnamus* [in which his aforementioned treatise against Peter Lombard's opinions is condemned].[231]

He wrote numerous works on the sacred scriptures, including: *On the Prophet Jeremiah,* in one book; *On the Prophet Daniel,* in one book; *On the Gospel of John,* in one book; *On the Apocalypse of John,* in one book; *On the Burdens [of Office],* to Henry VI, in one book; *On the Seven Seals,* in one book; *On Concordances,* in one book; *On the Fifteen Pontiffs,* in one book; an *Apologia,* to Pope Innocent [III], in one book; and certain other works that remain unknown to me.

This Joachim was considered to be a prophet in his own time and prognosticated many things concerning the future. [Indeed,] in all his works, he strives to discern the course of future times.

Joachim flourished under Henry V or Henry VI,[232] in the year of our Lord 1170.[233]

§118. Otto, Abbot

Otto, an abbot, was of distinguished education in the sacred learning, keen of mind, prompt in his knowledge, and skillful in his speech. He wrote works that are well worth reading. His principal productions include some notable sermons and homilies to the brethren, in one book; *On the Canon of the Mass,* in one

231. The Latin text in this paragraph (which is a single sentence in the original) is somewhat cumbersome to render in English, though its meaning is perfectly clear. It has been freely paraphrased here, to convey accurately its sense in (fairly) readable English.

232. This statement may reflect Trithemius's uncertainty about the times of the reigns of Henry V and Henry IV or his uncertainty concerning the ordinal nomenclature of the emperor concerned. In *De Scriptoribus Ecclesiasticis,* it is stated that he flourished under Henry VI. Trithemius, *De Scriptoribus Ecclesiasticis,* 88.

233. Joachim of Fiore is believed to have lived from about 1135 until 1202.

book; and a *Disputation with a Jew,* which he wrote to Wilbodon, a monk at Hasslingen, in one book.

He produced many others works, but these have not come to my notice. Many affirm that this Otto, after his abbacy, became the bishop of the church of Cambrai.

§119. Hildegard of Bingen

Hildegard, a holy nun, was the first abbess of the convent of Rupertsberg, at Bingen in the diocese of Mainz. She was born in the county of Sponheim and was a student of blessed Jutta, the countess of that place, in the convent of Disibodenberg. She was a virgin of holy life, who shone forth with many miracles while she lived.

I would not have included her in my present catalogue of authors, unless the authority of the supreme pontiff Eugene III had animated me to do so. For he approved of the works that Hildegard had written in the convent at Trier. These he had read before the public, in the presence of St. Bernard of Clairvaux and many cardinals and bishops. This is just as I remember myself to have said in my book *On Ecclesiastical Writers,* where I also provided another reason that impelled me [to include her in this catalogue].[234]

This virgin was illuminated by many divine revelations, as a result of which she composed a great quantity of volumes. These include: *Questions on the Rule of St. Benedict,* in one book; *On Thirty Questions,* to the monk Guibert, in one book; a *Life of St. Disibod, Bishop,* in one book; *Fifty-Eight Homilies on the Sunday Gospels,* in one book; *On the Sacrament of the Altar, against the Cathars,* in one book; the *Scivias* or *On the Knowledge of the*

---

234. The "other reason" to which Trithemius refers here is the fact that several popes (Eugene II, Anastasius IV, Hadrian IV, and Alexander III) had corresponded with Hildegard and commended the Roman Church to her prayers. Trithemius, *De Scriptoribus Ecclesiasticis,* 91. It seems curious that he should mention here this "other reason" here but not specify what it was. Moreover, his description of himself as "having remembering himself to have said" (*dixisse me memini*) may well indicate that he no longer had a copy of *De Scriptoribus Ecclesiasticis* in his possession to consult. Perhaps the "other reason" he mentions had simply slipped from his otherwise retentive memory.

Ways of God and Humans (a large and wondrous volume!), in one book; *The Merits of Life,* in three books; *Divine Works,* in one book; *Simple Medicines,* in one book; *Composite Medicines,* in one book; *On Future Perils in the Church,* to the clergy of Cologne, in one book; and a treatise on the same subject, to the clergy of Trier, in one book.

In this last-mentioned work, Hildegard predicted a future disaster for the church [at Trier] that was impending soon, because of the iniquities of the clergy; which [she said] could be averted only by means of penance. She was personally present in Trier [at that time], having been sent by the Lord. When she predicted this looming evil for the church because of the sins of its priests, all the clergy earnestly inquired of her, "Tell us, O lady, in what way we have offended God, that we should thus incur such dreadful wrath?" To this question, Hildegard responded with the memorable words, "[Believe me! For]the Holy Spirit does not mislead [those whom he inspires to prophesy!]" And all that she had predicted did indeed come to pass. For, from the year of our Lord 1185, the church of Trier, under the archbishop Volmar, was grievously afflicted with the scourge of dire schism for some seven years.

Hildegard wrote a practical exhortation to certain priests, in one book; [an exhortation] to her sisters, in one book; and a consoling discourse[235] to the monks of the monastery at Erbach.[236] She wrote many letters to various persons, numbering some 136, collected in one book; numerous songs and canticles, with sweet and marvelous melodies; and a work *On the Vices and Virtues,* in the form of a dialogue. She also wrote certain other minor, but nonetheless instructive, tracts.

Hildegard flourished in the year of our Lord 1160.[237]

---

235. Latin: *paregoricon.*

236. A town in southern Germany.

237. Hildegard is believed to have lived from about 1098 until 1179.

§120. Elizabeth of Schönau

Elizabeth, a nun and abbess in convent of Schönau in the diocese of Trier, was a virgin of the most exemplary sanctity. She received many revelations from God. For the sake of their usefulness in the edification of the faithful, she committed some of these to writing, composing the following volumes: *The Ways of God*, a noteworthy and useful work, in one book; *On the Revelation of Eleven Thousand Virgins of Cologne*, in one book; and her own *Revelations*, in three books. She also wrote a considerable number of letters to various people.

Let no future reader raise an objection that I am including women among this catalogue of the illustrious writers of our order! For in doing so, I am not without precedents among the earlier authorities. For blessed Isidor of Seville included Proba, the wife of the proconsul Adelphus, in his book *On Illustrious Persons*, because of the Virgilian centones which Proba wrote (although, indeed, this attribution seems to have been apocryphal). Certainly the holy virgins of our own order, who are consecrated to Christ, should not be considered in any way inferior to this married woman, Proba.

Elizabeth of Schönau lived at the same time as Hildegard, of whom she was a beloved friend and whose monastery was only about three miles from hers. More details of the life of Elizabeth are provided in her entry in the third book of the present work.[238] She died before Hildegard, in the year of our Lord 1165, in the thirteenth indiction, at the age of thirty-six, on the eighteenth day of June. She is buried in the Church of St. Florinus.

§121. Eckebert, Abbot

Eckebert was abbot of the monastery of St. Florinus at Schönau, within the boundaries of the diocese of Trier. He was the brother of blessed Elizabeth, the abbess of the convent of nuns in the

---

238. Trithemius, *De Viris Illustribus* 3.335.

same location, of whom we have already made mention.[239] Eckebert had been a canon at the church at Bonn. But, in response to the admonition of his sister, he renounced the world and became a monk at the monastery of the aforementioned monastery, under its first abbot, Hildelin.

When Hildelin passed away, Eckebert was constituted as abbot in his place. He was studious and learned in the sacred writings, and well educated also in secular literature. He excelled in composing both poetry and prose and was particularly gifted in delivering homilies and sermons.

Eckebert wrote [many works, including:] *Against Heresies,* in one book; *On the Prologue of the Gospel of John,* in one book; *On the Verse in the Gospel of Luke "An Angel was Sent,"* in one book; *On the Magnificat,* in one book; many elegant sermons, through the whole course of the year, [collected together] in one book; and a reflection upon the death of his sister [Elizabeth]. He wrote many letters to various persons, as well as prayers and poems. Eckebert also produced other works, which have not come to my notice.

His erudition and eloquence were so great that he overcame a certain heretic, Cardens, who held and cunningly taught a certain wicked and false doctrine on the body and blood of Christ. He achieved this in the very first debate, which was held in the presence of many learned men.

Then, in the year of our Lord 1163, in the eleventh indiction, on August 2 (which was a Friday), Eckebert defeated in a debate three other heresiarchs, known as Cataphrigas or Cathars—namely, Arnold, Marsilium, and Theoderic. He overcame them so convincingly that they were left quite incapable of offering any response to his arguments. But when these men stubbornly persisted in their pernicious errors, they were burned to death, together with six other men and two women. This took place outside the city gates, near the cemetery of the Jews, which is called the Jewish Hill.

239. See §120.

[In addition to such public disputations,] Eckebert also wrote various tracts against the [Cathar] heresy. He flourished in the year of our Lord 1170. [240]

§122. Peter of Cluny[241]

Peter, an abbot of the monastery at Cluny, was learned in the holy writings and well informed also in the secular disciplines. He was renowned both for his intelligence and eloquence, and no less venerable for his devotion and moral integrity than for his knowledge. He composed elegant and useful sermons for his brethren, compiled in one book. [He wrote also] *On the Solitary Life,* in one book; and letters to various persons, [compiled] in one book.

Peter also recorded in writing miracles and revelation which occurred during his times, of which many people possess copies. He wrote other works also, which I have not seen.[242]

§123. Hélinand,[243] Monk

Hélinand, a monk of Froidmont in the territory of Beauvais, was a most learned man in the divine writings and magnificently erudite in secular literature. He was of a subtle but fervent disposition, skillful in his speech, and distinguished by his handsome appearance.[244] And he was no less admirable for his [merits of] life than for his knowledge.

Hélinand produced several works in which his expertise in all fields is well displayed, namely; an outstanding and large volume of *Histories,* in forty-eight books; *On the Reparation of Those Who Have Fallen,* in one book; a considerable number of varied

240. Eckebert is believed to have died in 1184.

241. This Peter is generally known as Peter the Venerable.

242. Peter the Venerable is believed to have lived from about 1092 until 1156.

243. Trithemius gives the name of this writer as *Helmandus.*

244. Latin: *venusto lepore decorus.*

sermons; and letters to various persons. Of the other items he wrote, I have been able to discover nothing.

Hélinand flourished in the year of our Lord 1020.[245]

§124. William, Monk of Paris

William, a monk of the monastery of St. Dionysius in Paris, was studious and well versed in the divine writings and by no means ignorant of secular literature. He wrote a great work of the histories of past times, in three books. He is said to have produced commentaries on certain books of the Bible and various other writings; but these have not come into our hands.

§125. Simon, Monk

Simon, a monk of the monastery at Hasslingen, applied himself thoroughly to the study of sacred writings and was rich in his knowledge of the works of the ancient authorities. He made an abridged version of blessed Pope Gregory's *Moralia on Job*, presenting the moral principles [of Gregory] against the pertinent texts [of the book of Job]—thus expounding the entire volume [of Job] in different words.

Simon wrote elegant sermons and a commentary on the Song of Songs, in one book. He is said to have produced other works, which have not come into our hands.

§126. William, Abbot

William, abbot of the monastery at Poitiers, was learned and studious in the divine writings and knowledgeable also in secular

---

245. Hélinand is believed to have been born in about 1150. The year of his death is given by different sources as 1223, 1229, or 1237. In *De Scriptoribus Ecclesiasticis,* the year of his flourishing is given as 1200, suggesting that the 1020 that appears here (and is found in both the 1575 and 1605 editions) is a scribal or typographical error, and that 1200 is intended. This would be consistent with the approximately chronological ordering of authors. See Trithemius, *De Scriptoribus Ecclesiasticis,* 93.

literature. He was an outstanding theologian and jurist, and is said to have written a notable volume on the sacraments in which his abundant intelligence is well displayed.[246] He is said also to have written other works, but these have not come to my notice.

§127. Henry, Monk

Henry, a monk of the monastery at Hasslingen, was born in the city of Brussels in Brabant. He was studious and learned in the divine scriptures and of outstanding education in the arts of the humanities. He was also a great performer of calculations and computations.

Henry wrote a treatise on computation and a book on the calendar, which is extremely useful and highly erudite. He is said also to have written other works, but these have not come into our hands. He flourished in the year of our Lord 1200.

§128. Theodoric, Abbot

Theodoric, a German by birth, was an abbot in the diocese of Mainz. He was an educated and eloquent man. He wrote, for the edification of his readers, a life of that admirable virgin of Christ Hildegard of Bingen (of whom we have made mention previously),[247] in four books. He is said to have written other works, but these have not come into our hands. Theodoric flourished in the year of our Lord 1200.

§129. Philipp, Monk

Philipp of Bergamo, prior of the monastery of St. Mary of Avantia in Padua, was learned in the divine writings and of distinguished

---

246. This reference to a notable volume on the sacraments calls to mind the important and widely circulated work *De sacramento altaris,* of William of Saint-Thierry. It seems not impossible that the writer referred to here is this William (who was not, however, abbot of Poitiers but of Saint-Thierry.)

247. See §119.

education in secular literature. He was delightful, direct and clear in his expression, and produced works that are well worth reading. Of these works, I have seen seen only his sizeable and significant volume *On the Ethics of Cato*, in one book. Of the other works he is said to have written, I have seen nothing.

§130. Bernard of Montecassino

Bernard, an abbot of Montecassino, was studious and learned in the sacred scriptures and a zealous lover of the discipline of the monastic rule. He was of keen intellect, ready in giving counsel, firm in his opinions, and clear and skillful in his expression. He wrote a number of distinguished works. Of these, I have been able to find the following: *On the Rule of St. Benedict*, in one book; a *Mirror of Monks*, in one book; and a treatise on whether all [matters of monastic life] fall under the precept of the rule [of St. Benedict]. The other works that he wrote have not come to my notice.[248]

§131. Peter of Poitiers, Monk

Peter Berthorius of Poitiers was a monk and prior of the monastery of St. Eligius in Paris.[249] He was extremely studious in the divine scriptures and well informed also concerning secular literature. He wrote many praiseworthy works, in which his abundant talents are displayed.

[His works include the following scriptural commentaries:] *On Genesis*, in one book: *On Exodus*, in one book; *On Leviticus*, in one book; *On Numbers*, in one book; *On Deuteronomy*, in one book; *On Joshua*, in one book; *On Judges*, in one book; *On Ruth*, in one book; *On the Books of Kings*, in four books; *On the Books of Chronicles*, in two books; *On Esdras and Nehemiah*, in three

248. This Bernard is the same person as Bernard Ayglerius (also known as Bernardus Cassinensis), who wrote a commentary on the Rule of St. Benedict and a work entitled *Speculum monachorum*. He is believed to have lived from 1216 until 1282 and is sometimes identified as a cardinal.

249. The author referred to in this entry is generally known as Pierre Bersuire, or Petrus Berchorius. He is believed to have lived from 1290 until 1362.

books; *On Tobit,* in one book; *On Judith,* in one book; *On Esther,* in one book; *On Job,* in one book; *On Isaiah,* in one book; *On Jeremiah,* in one book; *On Ezekiel,* in nine books; *On Daniel,* in one book; *On the Twelve Minor Prophets,* in twelve books; *On the Books of Maccabees,* in two books; *On the Gospel of Matthew,* in one book; *On the Gospel of Mark,* in one book; *On the Gospel of Luke,* in one book; *On the Gospel of John,* in one book; *On the Letters of Paul,* in fourteen books; *On the Canonical Epistles,* in seven books; *On the Acts of the Apostles,* in one book; and *On the Apocalypse of John,* in one book.

He wrote a great work in three volumes, to which he gave the title *A Moral Repertory,* which some others refer to as the [moral] dictionary. He also wrote *Moral Interpretations,*[250] in three volumes; and a *Moral Introduction,* in three volumes.

Peter Berthorius produced a brief *Summary of the Stories of the Bible,* in one book; as well as sermons, letters, and diverse other tracts, which have not come into our hands.

§132. Lapo, Abbot and Teacher

Lapo da Castiglionchio, abbot of St. Minia, was a most expert jurist in both fields of laws [that is, church and civil] and well educated in both human and divine literature.[251] He is said to have produced a number of works, demonstrating his capacities. Of these, I have been able to discover only the following: *On the Clementine Constitutions,*[252] in one book. None of his other writings have come my way. Lapo flourished in the year of our Lord 1340.[253]

---

250. Latin: *Morale reductorium.* This work presents moral interpretations of scripture as well as stories from Ovid's *Metamorphoses*—hence the English rendering of its title provided above.

251. Lapo da Castiglionchio was a prominent lawyer, who was burned to death in the Revolt of Ciompi in Florence. Contrary to Trithemius's description, he was not a Benedictine monk.

252. A collection of decretals, which formed part of *Corpus Juris Canonici.*

253. Lapo da Castiglionchio is believed to have lived from about 1316 until 1381.

§133. Pope Clement VI, Abbot

Pope Clement VI, previously known as Pierre Roger, had served as abbot of the monastery at Fécamp.[254] We shall make mention of him in the fourth book [of this present work].[255] He was a man of the highest learning in all disciplines, subtle in his intellect, clear in his expression, and truly outstanding as a preacher to the people. He wrote very polished sermons, which are highly esteemed by many, and numerous speeches on various subjects. He also wrote many other works. Clement VI flourished in the year of our Lord 1345.[256]

§134. Pierre Bohier,[257] Abbot

Pierre Bohier, abbot of the monastery of Aniane,[258] was a famous teacher of canon law in his time. He was learned in the divine writings, of brilliant intellect and profound knowledge, and precise in his speech. He produced numerous works that are not to be overlooked. Of these, I have seen the following: *A [Commentary] on the "Mirror of Monks" of Bernard of Montecassino,*[259] in one book; and *On the Signs of Speech for Monks,* in one book.

Pierre wrote a commentary on the rule of our holy father Benedict—a highly commendable work, involving much labor. In this volume, he demonstrates the rule [of St. Benedict] to accord perfectly with [church] laws and canons, virtually in every single word. The other works that he wrote have not come into our hands.

Pierre Bohier flourished in the year of our Lord 1350.[260]

254. In Normandy.

255. In this fourth book, Trithemius provides a catalogue of Benedictine popes, cardinals, archbishops, and bishops.

256. Clement VI is believed to have lived from 1291 until 1352.

257. Latin: *Petrus Boherii.*

258. In Hérault, France.

259. See §130.

260. Pierre Bohier is believed to have died around 1388.

§135. Johannes, Monk

Johannes, a monk of Kastl in the diocese of Eichstätt, was highly studious in the divine scriptures and by no means ignorant of secular literature. He was of keen intellect and an accomplished speaker. He produced a considerable number of volumes that are worthy of careful reading. These include: *On the Rule of Our Holy Father Benedict,* in two books; a compendious *summa* of the Bible, in one book; *Sermons on the Epistles and Gospel Readings throughout the Entire Cycle of the Year* (both for the liturgical seasons and the feasts of the saints), in two books; and *Forty-two Sermons on the Passion of the Lord.* He also left many letters to diverse persons and various other works, which have not come into our hands.[261]

§136. André,[262] Monk and Bishop

André [Dias de Escobar] was (as he himself writes in a certain one of his tracts) a monk of our order, who became bishop of Megara, then Ciudad Rodrigo, and finally Ajaccio.[263] He was a Spaniard by birth, an [apostolic] penitentiary of the Roman curia, an expert teacher of jurisprudence, and also well versed in the divine scriptures. He wrote: *On Penitence,* in one book; and *On the Manner and Form of Confession,* a brief but very useful tract. He wrote also many other works, which have not come into my hands.[264]

§137. Petrus, Monk of Melk

Petrus von Rosenheim, a monk of Melk Abbey in Austria, was studious in the divine writings and well instructed also in secular literature. He was proficient in composing both poetry and prose. At the request of master Nikolaus von Dinkelsbühl, he composed

261. Johannes von Kastl is believed to have died sometime after 1426.

262. Generally known as André Dias de Escobar.

263. André Dias de Escobar was first appointed as bishop of Ciudad Rodrigo (1410) and then Ajaccio (1422). His appointment as bishop of Megara (a titular see) actually followed his resignation from Ajaccio, in 1428.

264. André Dias de Escobar is believed to have lived from 1348 until 1448.

a metrical paraphrase of the entire Bible, dedicated to Branda,[265] cardinal of St. Clement's and apostolic legate. To this work, to which he gave the title of *A Roseate Memorial of Divine Eloquence*, he summarized whatever is contained in each chapter of scripture in two verses [of poetry]. He wrote also a historical chronicle, in one book; and letters, sermons, and diverse other tracts.

Petrus von Rosenheim flourished during the times of the Council of Constance, in the year of our Lord 1420.[266]

§138. Heinrich, Abbot

Heinrich von Gulpen, a German by birth, was the abbot of the monastery of St. Giles in Nuremburg and a learned teacher of canon law. No less venerable for his conduct of life than for his knowledge, his genius was praised by Johannes Nider in his *Formicarius*.[267]

He wrote works of considerable authority, including: *On Seven Distinctions Concerning Penitence*, in one book; *On a Distinction Concerning Consecration*, in one book; and *On the Passion of the Lord*, in one tract. If he wrote more than this, his other works have not come to my notice.

Heinrich von Gulpen flourished in the times of the Council of Basel, in the year of our Lord of our Lord 1430.[268]

§139. Nicolò of Palermo

Nicolò [de' Tudeschi], a Sicilian by birth, served as abbot of the monastery at Maniace[269] before becoming archbishop of Palermo and a cardinal of the holy Roman Church. He was a man of the

265. I.e., Branda Castiglione.

266. Petrus von Rosenheim is believed to have lived from 1380 until 1433.

267. The *Formicarius* (Ant colony) of Johannes Nider was a treatise written in the form of a dialogue discussing the workings of Christian society, first published in 1475.

268. Heinrich von Gulpen is believed to have died in 1435.

269. Near Messina.

highest expertise in both laws [ecclesiastical and civil]. A prudent interpreter of uncertain questions, he was held in the highest esteem and authority by jurists. He wrote numerous outstanding volumes. Of these, I have been able to find the following: *On the Clementine Constitutions,* in one book; and *On the Sixth Decretal,*[270] in one book. He began to write a [critical] apparatus to [Gratian's] *Decretum* but never completed it.

[He also compiled a volume of] many counsels, some 104 in number, in one book; and *On the Order of Judges,* in one book. He wrote a notable and lengthy tract affirming the authority of the Council of Basel, which was publicly read before the leaders and clergy of Frankfurt. He produced also [accounts of] various [canonical] disputations and records [of cases and deliberations]. But these have not come into our hands.

[Nicolò de' Tudeschi] flourished during the times of the Council of Basel, in the year of our Lord 1435.[271]

§140. Johannes Rode, Abbot

Johannes Rode, a German by birth, was abbot of the monastery of St. Matthew the apostle, outside the city of Trier. He was a most expert teacher of [canon] law and extremely studious in the divine writings. Outstanding for his sanctity of life and conduct, he was a zealous observer of the disciplines of the monastic rule. He applied himself diligently to the restoration of the regular observance in the aforementioned monastery [of St. Matthew] and achieved good progress in this regard.

In clear language, he wrote constitutions that were necessary for the reformation of the order, and which were put into practice in his own monastery. He composed also a simple but very useful sermon on the leadership office of the abbot; and certain other works, for the edification of monks.

270. This, like the Clementine constitutions, was one of the compilations forming *Corpus Juris Canonici.*

271. Nicolò de' Tudeschi is believed to have lived from 1386 until 1445.

He had first been an official of the curia [of the archbishop] of Trier. After this, disdaining the world, he entered the Carthusian house in the same place. There he persevered in a laudable fashion for a number of years. But at last, with apostolic authority (procured through the archbishop of Trier), he entered our own order. He was then elected as abbot, for the purpose of reforming the monastery that he had joined.[272]

Johannes was a learned, zealous, and devout man, concerning whom no one ever entertained an adverse opinion. He departed from the Carthusians only for the honor of God and for the sake the restoration of our own order. He flourished in the times of the Council of Basel, in the year of our Lord 1435.[273]

§141. Andrew, Monk

Andrew, originally from Utrecht, was a monk of our own monastery at Sponheim—where, by the will of God, I myself serve (admittedly, in useless fashion!). He had studied the sacred scriptures thoroughly and was well trained also in secular literature. Proficient in both poetry and prose, he was of delightful speech and distinguished by his handsome appearance. [274]

Andrew wrote some short works, which are well worth reading. These include the following: a *Soliloquy of the Human Being to God*, in one book; *On the Progress of the Virtues*, in one book; *On When the Consumption of Meat Is Permissible for Monks*, in one book; and *On the Use of Wool* [*in Monastic Clothing*], to the abbot of the monastery of St. Mary at Trier, in one book. He also composed many letters to various persons, collations, and diverse poems. He flourished in the year of our Lord 1440.

272. The version of the life of Johannes Rode presented in *De Scriptoribus Ecclesiasticis* indicates that the archbishop of Trier took him from the Carthusian monastery (where he had served as prior) to reform the Benedictine monastery of St. Matthew, as well as other Benedictine houses in his diocese. Trithemius, *De Scriptoribus Ecclesiasticis*, 172.

273. Johannes Rode is believed to have died in 1439.

274. Latin: *pulchro venustatis lepore compositus*.

§142. Conrad, Abbot of St. John

Conrad von Rodenburg served as abbot of the monastery at Johannisberg in the Rheingau. He was a devout man and an ardent lover of the newly introduced [reformed] observance of the monastic rule. He was studious in the divine writings and a distinguished orator in his time. He wrote numerous works in a straightforward and open style, which are useful to read.

Among these works is a lengthy and impressive tract on the praises of the Blessed Mary, ever virgin, of whom he was a great devotee. In this book, which he entitled *The Vine of the Lord Sabaoth*, he weaves the praises of Mary by considering each of her members under the figure of a grapevine.

He wrote also a volume of devout exercises for the instruction of novices, in one book; and a brief tract, *On the Approach to the Altar*. He made many noteworthy compilations, drawing upon the writings from the fathers from various places.

Conrad von Rodenburg was one of those who prepared [revised] directions and ceremonies, following the reformation [of monastic observance] in our own times, at the command of the fathers [of the Bursfelde congregation].

He died an old man, full of days, on the twenty-fifth day of December, in the year of our Lord 1486, in the fourth indiction.

§143. Nicolaus Donis,[275] Monk

Nicolaus Donis, a German by birth, was a monk of our order. His monastery does not spring to my memory at this point. He was remarkably learned in secular literature and is greatly admired as a cosmographer in our own times. He produced a work for the supreme pontiff, Paul II, *On Cosmography*, in eight books. This volume, the product of much labor, features illustrations of the tables of Ptolemy. He also wrote *On Certain Places and Marvels of the World*, in one book; and certain other works, which I have not

---

275. Often referred to as Nicolaus Germanus.

seen. Nicolaus Donis flourished under Paul II and Sixtus IV, in the year of our Lord 1480. He died only seven years ago.[276]

276. This would place the year of Nicolaus's death at about 1485. Other sources give 1490 as the approximate year of his death.

A note that not all the authors of our order have been included in this catalogue, because of their great multitude

Let no one imagine that the monks and fathers whom we have named in this book were the only one who have shed luster upon the order of our holy father Benedict through their learning and writings. Indeed, we have left out many great authors, because of the sheer multitude of them. For neither sufficient leisure time is available to us nor the opportunity of inserting all those whom we have omitted.

Who could doubt that there are many other outstanding persons of our order of whom we would have made mention here, if their times, lives, and dignities had been known to us? The order founded by our lawgiver [Benedict] has continued for some nine hundred years and during that time has never been without highly educated persons in all fields of learning. But we are not able to make mention of them all, of course, since their names are not known to us. They did not write out of ambition or for the sake of perpetuating the fame of their names, as so many do [today]; but rather for the glory of God and for the salvation of souls.

And for the love of God, they would [often] humbly omit their own names from their works. But useful material remains efficacious, even when the name of the author is not given. However, such is the foolishness[1] of persons of our own age that, unless the name of the author is known, then the writings are dismissed as inconsequential.

---

1. Latin: *curiositas.*

Otherwise, we have included a selection of but a few out of many. Yet in doing this, we believe that we have done no injury to anyone, even if there are brilliant persons, unknown to us, whom we have passed over in silence. [The same applies] if we have described certain writers differently from how others would wish.

Indeed, I know that many abbots and brothers of our order claim as their own learned authors of other [orders or monasteries], in order to gain greater prestige for their own monasteries. To demonstrate the truth of this, I shall give a single example. I will briefly relate what certain persons (whose names I shall not mention) say concerning Haymo. Now, Haymo was a monk of the monastery at Fulda who became the third bishop of Halberstadt, as we have stated above.[2] Nevertheless, I know of three different monasteries who each claim him as their own. And two of these monasteries were not even founded until two or three centuries after Haymo's death! How is it supposed to be that he, who lived so many years before they were even founded, could have been a monk of their monastery? It is a ridiculous business, which arises [only out of the desire for] prestige in the eyes of others. Hence it is that I have said that no one should imagine that I have done them an injury, if I have [seemed to] assign one of their own learned writers (as they see it) to another monastery.

I have often examined many histories and chronicles with the greatest diligence, as much as has been possible to me. I have labored hard in this way lest, deceived by false opinions, I should offer falsehoods in place of the truth. Nevertheless, I am a mortal and not an angel, and flesh and not spirit; and thus I am able to be misled and hence [unwittingly and unwillingly] to mislead others. [In many cases,] I do not assert my own judgments but rather simply acquiesce to the opinions of others, when these seem probable. If anyone should detect any error in my work, I willingly defer to those who possess sounder knowledge.

While my efforts [in preparing this work] have been not inconsiderable, I do not dare to assert that they have been entirely sufficient. For in the great variety of histories, there is a great

2. See §34.

diversity of opinions on many matters. If anyone desires to learn of more writers from our order, they may read the records of the old authors. But we, as far as our other duties have permitted, have written about a few [of our Benedictine authors], for the glory of our order. [In doing this, I intend to] present an opportunity and invitation for my future readers—that if there is anyone who loves the praises of our tradition, they may add yet more illustrious writers whom they discover, and find not to be included in our present catalogue.

A final exhortation to the members of our order, that they apply themselves to the study of sacred writings

At the end of this second book of my work, it is fitting that I say a few things to all those who, under the rule of our holy father Benedict, occupy the earth in an unfruitful and profitless manner. Such persons fail to imitate the examples of their noble predecessors in our order—though they could well do so, if they chose! There are many who are pleased to hear the praises of our order being extolled. But they refuse to take any notice when they themselves are encouraged to follow in the footsteps of those persons of past times whom they acknowledge to be praiseworthy.

Believe me, fathers and brothers, it was not idleness that made our order so glorious but labor, vigilance, and study! To give a brief summary of the glory of our tradition, there are two things that brought our order to the heights of honor—namely, merit of sanctity and literary culture. When these died away, then that which had once stood so strongly collapsed heavily. If we wish to return our order (or even part of it) to its pristine state, it behooves us to love both sanctity of life and the learning of wisdom. Neither is it possible for good discipline to be preserved in our order if either sanctity of life or the authority of sacred learning is absent. Towering monastery buildings, great financial incomes, and ample possessions of land are *not* what create stable discipline in our order.

Rather, we must return to the study of sacred reading, following the example of our predecessors. Thus divinely illuminated, we shall be able to progress in virtue and sanctity, and, indeed, increase the glory of our order by our own studies. Let each one apply themselves diligently, according to the grace given to them by heaven. All should instruct themselves usefully, and all should apply their diligence to the cultivation of salubrious knowledge. "The hand of the Lord has not been shortened,"[1] such that God would deny to us what he once bestowed so liberally upon [our Benedictine forebears]. All that is required of us is to offer thanks to God, by means of our goodwill and study.

Behold, now all things smile opportunely upon those who pursue learning! For the new invention of the art of printing has brought many thousands of books to light. Today, for the cost of but a little money, anyone is able to become educated. Happy indeed is this [present] age, which has merited such a gift from God!

In the past there was a great paucity of books, which could be produced only with considerably expense and labor. But now there is a vast abundance of volumes of all varieties of writings. By means of these, anyone is able to acquire knowledge of literature easily. Why, brethren, do you neglect such a necessary thing? Why do you languish in inert idleness? Why do you disdain this singular blessing that is offered to you?

Or do you imagine that anyone is able to gain virtue without labor or to acquire knowledge without study? Consider those of whom we have made mention in this catalogue and how they progressed astonishingly in their knowledge of all branches of literature. Know that there is no study without love, and no knowledge without effort, and no victory without a battle! But this labor [though sometimes difficult] has this solace—that it inflames divine love. These [Benedictine writers of the past] were people like us—mortal, frail, and subject to the passions. But the grace of God was victorious within them, and their love of scriptures overcame the recalcitrance of the flesh. They knew full well that anyone who loves literary studies does not also love the vices of the flesh. They realized that there is nothing that is more sweetly attained, nothing that is more happily or more securely possessed, and nothing that so effectively retracts the mind from carnal pleasure, as true love and knowledge of literature.

1. Isa 59:1.

This, O brethren, is the honorable mother who loves those who love her and who has exalted our order since its very beginnings. Oh, if only you knew how much honor and usefulness there is in the love of learning! Then you would never tire of its cultivation.

Would you like me to say briefly what I believe about sacred studies? Then hear me. A monk who is a lover of the sacred writings is like a lion, the strongest of all beasts, who fears no enemies. And why? Because this holy learning is "like the tower of David, built as an armory, from which hangs a thousand shields, the arms of all the strong."[2] It contains within itself such virtue and strength that it renders all those who love it almost invincible, while it liberates their minds from all earthly allurements.

[This holy learning] gives to those who love it constancy in tribulation, patience in adversity, and humility in victory. It infuses the love of God into the hearts of the faithful and inspires reverence and fear in the minds of the proud. If it finds a person worthy of itself, it makes them utterly free from all servitude. It teaches them to flee the vices, to love the virtues, to disdain what is earthly, to long for that which is heavenly, and to love God above all else.

And when [such a person] loves nothing of this earth, then they are not saddened by the loss of anything. This is true freedom: to make one's soul a stranger to all earthly affections! To this freest of all liberties, sacred scripture summons us and forms us, if it is studied with sincerity of love.

O Lord, how sweet is your spirit, which is imbibed in the purity of a humble heart inflamed with love of the holy writings! Such a person is able to love nothing earthly nor to desire any passing thing. The whole affection of their mind is raised upwards with burning longing; all their efforts are grounded in the love of God. It is literature, indeed, that arouses us to devotion when we are languishing, inflames the mind to love of God, generates disdain for present things, and subdues the voluptuous stirrings of the flesh.

If you love [sacred learning] with all your heart, it will honor you. If you cultivate it, it shall exalt you! Without it, human life is

2. Song 4:4.

but [a seeking for fleshly] pleasure or a vain futility. And yet we still remain as we are! Whether monk or abbot, is there anyone who, unless they love holy learning, is able to delight in anything but vanities? Indeed, unless the heart is delightfully occupied in sacred studies, it is inevitable that it will be enmeshed in vanities and so become foully stained. Hence it is that our abbots, not applying themselves to holy learning, are filled with ambition for earthly things. They seek futile riches, they desire false honors, and they immerse themselves totally in secular concerns.

For it is necessary for their intentions and affections to be focused on *something,* be it good or bad. The human heart is not able to be without its aspirations and desires, as long as we are alive. Anyone who refuses to be occupied in sacred studies will (without doubt) come to be occupied with other things, which are contrary to them. Hence some [members of the Order of St. Benedict] occupy themselves with carriages and horses, while others concern themselves with riches and splendid buildings. Then there are those who give themselves over to feasting and drinking, and others who occupy themselves with games and vain pastimes. And yet others find their delights in the "business of women."[3]

Indeed, there are few who can preserve well in the clerical or monastic life, unless they have a love of holy learning. Many are called, but, truly, few are chosen! Those who [really] know the sacred writings [always] come to love them. For such learning has no enemies, except for those who are ignorant of it.

Considering the ancient splendor of our noble order, let us take care to apply our souls to the holy studies. In this way, by exerting ourselves in good labors, we shall merit to possess their reward—namely, eternal life!

THE END

3. Latin: *mulierum factis delectantur.* This may signify womanizing, or it may refer to the pursuit of interests that were seen as feminine (e.g., concern with clothing and grooming, etc.). The present translation is intended to retain something of that ambiguity.

Bibliography

Arnold, Klaus. *Johannes Trithemius: 1462–1516.* Würzburg, Germ.: Schöningh, 1991.

Brann, Noël L. *The Abbot Trithemius: The Renaissance of Monastic Humanism.* Studies in the History of Christian Thought. Leiden, Neth.: Brill, 1981.

Busaeus, Johannes. "Historica Relatio de Ioannis Trithemii Vita, Moribus et Scriptis." In *Opera Pia et Spirituales*, edited by Johannes Trithemius, unnumbered prefatory pages. Mainz, Germ.: Albinus, 1605.

Godelmann, Johann Georg. *Tractatus de Magis, Veneficis et Lamiis Recte Cognoscendis et Puniendis.* Frankfurt: Saurius, 1601.

Duraclus, Johannes. "Pinax sive Index Lucubrationum Joannis Trithemii." In *Libri Polygraphiae 6*, edited by Johannes Trithemius, 4–13. Cologne: Birkmann and Richwin, 1564.

Heidel, Wolfgang Earnest. "Epistola Dedicatoria Damiano Hartardo." In *Steganographia Vindicata, Reserata et Illustrata*, edited by Johannes Trithemius, unnumbered prefatory pages. Nuremberg: Rüdiger, 1721.

———. "Vita Joannis Trithemii." In *Steganographia Vindicata, Reserata et Illustrata*, edited by Johannes Trithemius, unnumbered prefatory pages. Nuremberg: Rüdiger, 1721.

Kloss, Georg Franz Burkhard. *Catalogue of the Library of Dr. Kloss of Franckfort, Vol. 12.* London: Sotheby and Son, 1835.

Torquemada, Juan de, et al. *Regula S. Benedicti cum Doctissimis and Piissimis Commentariis.* Cologne: Calenius, 1575.

Trithemius, Johannes. *Antipalus Maleficiorum.* Mainz, Germ.: Lippius, 1605.

———. "Chronicon Monasterii Sancti Jacobi." In *Opera Pia et Spirituales*, edited by Johannes Trithemius, 1–17. Mainz, Germ.: Albinus, 1605.

———. *De Laude Scriptorum Manualium.* Mainz, Germ.: Friedberg, 1494.

———. *De Scriptoribus Ecclesiasticis.* Paris: Rembolt, 1494.

———. *De Septem Secunda Deis id est Intelligentiis sive Spiritibus Moventibus Orbes.* Frankfurt: Jacobus, 1545.

———. *De Viris Illustribus Ordinis Sancti Benedicti.* In *Regula S. Benedicti cum Doctissimis and Piissimis Commentariis*, edited by Juan de Torquemada et al., 427–535. Cologne: Calenius, 1575.

———. *De Viris Illustribus Ordinis Sancti Benedicti.* In *Opera Pia et Spirituales*, edited by Johannes Trithemius, 17–149. Mainz, Germ.: Albinus, 1605.

———. *Libri Polygraphiae 6.* Strasbourg: Zetzner, 1613.

———. *The Magical Amulets of the Ancient Sages and Bibliotheca Necromantica.* Translated by Robert Nixon. Yorkshire: Hadean, 2023.

———. "The Magic and Philosophy of Trithemius of Spanheim, Containing His Book of Secret Things." In *The Magus, or Celestial Intelligencer,* edited and translated by Francis Barret, 131–40. London: Lackington, Allen and Company, 1801.

———. *Steganographia.* Darmstadt, Germ.: Berner, 1621.

———. *Veterum Sophorum Sigilla et Imagines Magicae.* Herrnstadt, Germ. [Wąsosz, Pol.]: Roth, 1732.

Voragine, Jacobus de, et al. *St. Benedict's Bones: A Medieval Monastic Mystery.* Translated by Robert Nixon. Eugene, OR: Resource, 2022.